'FIFA is world class at making money – but then what? If there's one man who can answer that question, it's Alan Tomlinson.'
Brian Oliver, former sports editor of
The Observer

'I have been reading Alan Tomlinson for over twenty years. This new work is well-researched, insightful and a testimony to the troubles that unfortunately still exist in sport today.'
Steven Berryman, sports corruption investigator

'Professor Alan Tomlinson's long-standing scholarship has been a beacon for those of us who have tried to challenge the culture of secrecy and impunity surrounding global football governance. *What Is FIFA For?* is a clear-eyed examination of an organization that has too often drifted far from the values it proclaims – integrity, fair play and transparency. As someone who has lived through some of FIFA's darker corners, I read Alan Tomlinson's latest work as both a warning and a call to action. If you care about the future of football, it is essential reading.'
Bonita Mersiades, Fair Play Publishing

'FIFA sets the rules of the game but, in today's commercialized environment, it does much more besides. This book asks: should it?'
Stephen Weatherill, University of Oxford

'A compelling and timely exploration of football's most influential governing body. Professor Alan Tomlinson brings his unparalleled expertise and investigative acumen to deliver a rigorous, balanced and insightful analysis to unpack FIFA's political dynamics, commercial strategies and persistent challenges around corruption and ethics. This book asks the hard questions about integrity, fair play and accessibility, making it essential reading for anyone who cares about the future of football.'
Louise Mansfield, Brunel University London

The status quo is broken. The world is grappling with a web of challenges that could threaten our very existence. If we believe in a better world, now is the time to question the purpose behind our actions and those taken in our name.

Enter the What Is It For? series – a bold exploration of the core elements shaping our world, from religion and free speech to animal rights and war. This series cuts through the noise to reveal the true impact of these topics, what they really do and why they matter.

Ditching the usual heated debates and polarizations, this series offers fresh, forward-thinking insights. Leading experts present groundbreaking ideas and point to ways forward for real change, urging us to envision a brighter future.

Each book dives into the history and function of its subject, uncovering its role in society and, crucially, how it can be better.

Series editor: George Miller

Visit **bristoluniversitypress.co.uk/what-is-it-for** to find out more about the series.

Available now

WHAT ARE ANIMAL RIGHTS FOR?
Steve Cooke

WHAT IS COUNTERTERRORISM FOR?
Leonie Jackson

WHAT IS CYBERSECURITY FOR?
Tim Stevens

WHAT IS DRUG POLICY FOR?
Julia Buxton

WHAT IS FIFA FOR?
Alan Tomlinson

WHAT IS HISTORY FOR?
Robert Gildea

WHAT IS HUMANISM FOR?
Richard Norman

WHAT IS IMMIGRATION POLICY FOR?
Madeleine Sumption

WHAT IS JOURNALISM FOR?
Jon Allsop

WHAT IS THE MONARCHY FOR?
Laura Clancy

WHAT ARE MUSEUMS FOR?
Jon Sleigh

WHAT ARE NUCLEAR WEAPONS FOR?
Patricia Shamai

WHAT ARE THE OLYMPICS FOR?
Jules Boykoff

WHAT IS PHILANTHROPY FOR?
Rhodri Davies

WHAT ARE PRISONS FOR?
Hindpal Singh Bhui

WHAT IS TRUTH FOR?
N.J. Enfield

WHAT IS VEGANISM FOR?
Catherine Oliver

WHAT IS WAR FOR?
Jack McDonald

WHAT IS THE WELFARE STATE FOR?
Paul Spicker

WHAT ARE ZOOS FOR?
Heather Browning and Walter Veit

Forthcoming

WHAT IS ANARCHISM FOR?
Nathan Jun

WHAT IS ANTHROPOLOGY FOR?
Kriti Kapila

WHAT ARE CONSPIRACY THEORIES FOR?
James Fitzgerald

WHAT IS FREE SPEECH FOR?
Govan Titley

**WHAT IS INTERNATIONAL
        DEVELOPMENT FOR?**
Andrea Cornwall

WHAT ARE MARKETS FOR?
Phillip Roscoe

WHAT IS MUSIC FOR?
Fleur Brouwer

WHAT ARE THE POLICE FOR?
Ben Bradford

WHAT IS RELIGION FOR?
Malise Ruthven

WHAT IS RESILIENCE FOR?
Hamideh Mahdiani

WHAT IS SPACE EXPLORATION FOR?
Tony Milligan and Koji Tachibana

WHAT ARE STATUES FOR?
Milly Williamson

ALAN TOMLINSON is the author/co-author of several books on FIFA. These include *Sir Stanley Rous and the Growth of World Football: An Englishman Abroad* (Cambridge Scholars, 2020), *FIFA: The Men, the Myths and the Money* (Routledge, 2014), *Badfellas: FIFA Family at War* (with John Sugden, Mainstream, 2003) and *FIFA and the Contest for World Football: Who Rules the Peoples' Game?* (with John Sugden, Polity Press, 1998). His academic articles on FIFA have appeared in *Sociology of Sport Journal*, *Journal of Sport & Social Issues*, *Soccer and Society*, *The International Journal of the History of Sport*, the *Oxford Journal of Legal Studies* and numerous edited volumes. His journalistic pieces have appeared in *New Statesman*, *Financial Times*, *When Saturday Comes* and *Der Tagesspiegel*. Alan Tomlinson is Emeritus Professor of Leisure Studies at the University of Brighton, UK.

WHAT IS FIFA FOR?

ALAN TOMLINSON

First published in Great Britain in 2026 by

Bristol University Press
University of Bristol
1–9 Old Park Hill
Bristol
BS2 8BB
UK
t: +44 (0)117 374 6645
e: bup-info@bristol.ac.uk

Details of international sales and distribution partners are available at
bristoluniversitypress.co.uk

© Alan Tomlinson 2026

DOI: 10.51952/9781529245769

British Library Cataloguing in Publication Data
A catalogue record for this book is available from the British Library

ISBN 978-1-5292-4574-5 paperback
ISBN 978-1-5292-4575-2 ePub
ISBN 978-1-5292-4576-9 ePdf

The right of Alan Tomlinson to be identified as author of this work has been
asserted by him in accordance with the Copyright, Designs and Patents Act 1988.

All rights reserved: no part of this publication may be reproduced, stored in a
retrieval system, or transmitted in any form or by any means, electronic, mechanical,
photocopying, recording, or otherwise without the prior permission of Bristol
University Press.

Every reasonable effort has been made to obtain permission to reproduce copyrighted
material. If, however, anyone knows of an oversight, please contact the publisher.

The statements and opinions contained within this publication are solely those of the
author and not of the University of Bristol or Bristol University Press. The University
of Bristol and Bristol University Press disclaim responsibility for any injury to
persons or property resulting from any material published in this publication.

Bristol University Press works to counter discrimination on grounds
of gender, race, disability, age and sexuality.

Cover design: Tom Appshaw

For football followers and enthusiasts, worldwide

CONTENTS

List of Figures, Tables and Boxes		xv
Acknowledgements		xviii
1	**Introduction: FIFA – What's at Stake?**	1
2	**FIFA and the Making of the Modern Game**	9
3	**FIFA and its Members**	36
4	**FIFA and its Commercial Partners**	49
5	**'Good-looking Governance': Investigating Corruption**	71
6	**FIFA and the Americas**	86
7	**FIFA in Africa and Asia: Challenges and Constraints**	100
8	**FIFA and the Women's Game**	111
9	**A Law unto Itself?**	126

10 **Conclusion**	**138**
Notes	**147**
Further Reading	**161**
Index	**164**

LIST OF FIGURES, TABLES AND BOXES

Figures

2.1	Sepp Blatter, general secretary of FIFA, and João Havelange, president of FIFA, holding the Adidas Tango España, 1982 (Nationaal Archief Fotocollectie Anefo). Published under CC BY-SA 3.0 NL licence	25
2.2	Protest on Copacabana Beach, 10 June 2014, Brazil men's World Cup (photograph by the author)	28
2.3	The US Department of Justice's FIFAgraph – 'the Enterprise'	33
4.1	FIFA headquarters in Zurich (Rafael_Wiedenmeier, iStock)	52
4.2	Sports marketing bribery schemes (US Department of Justice)	57
4.3	Countries that have hosted the men's FIFA World Cup, 1930–2034 (map template source: Wikimedia Commons [public domain])	62
4.4	Countries that have won the men's FIFA World Cup, 1930–2022 (map template source: Wikimedia Commons [public domain])	64

6.1	Alan Rothenberg, smooth entrepreneur par excellence, relaxing in Hotel Le Bristol Paris at the France 1998 World Cup (photograph by Alys Tomlinson, reproduced with permission)	94
9.1	Chuck Blazer (photograph by Alys Tomlinson, reproduced with permission)	134
10.1	France 1938 – foot firmly on the ball, but Italy wins its second World Cup (poster by Henri Desmé, public domain)	141

Tables

2.1	FIFA's first nine presidents	23
4.1	Spectators at FIFA's first 15 men's World Cup Finals	65
4.2	Spectators at men's World Cup Finals, 1998–2022	66

Boxes

2.1	What was this institutional newcomer FIFA all about?	22
2.2	FIFA goes to Hollywood	30
3.1	'Say no to racism – my game is fair play'	47
7.1	Why the giant confederations need to regionalize – a football administrator's view	108
8.1	Women's soccer in the United States – 'ahead of the curve'	117

8.2	Women's football in Africa – contending with multiple problems	123
9.1	What is 'sports law'? Do governing bodies in sport make law or are they merely subject to it?	127

ACKNOWLEDGEMENTS

Thanks to innumerable individuals who have spoken to me about FIFA and its place in the history and politics of football over the last 40 years. It's pretty much impossible to specify each person who has made an influential contribution to my understanding of the place of FIFA in both its historical and its contemporary contexts. Countless people have offered perceptive insights on the topic, whether in written form, face-to-face encounters, or public debate and exchange. I thank them all and sincerely hope that I have not misrepresented views or experiences, though it is inevitable that interpretive interventions can in some circumstances be misunderstood. If that is the case anywhere in this book, I apologise in advance.

More specific thanks go to the three anonymous reviewers who were both objectively critical and supportive. The series editor, George Miller, has been hugely positive and helpful throughout the commissioning, writing and editing process. His tactful advice has curbed my adjectival excesses in particular, along with alerting me to my tendency to here and there fall into forms of academic verbosity!

The University of Brighton has continued to offer me support throughout the period of development and production of the book. I am especially grateful to the patient librarians at the Falmer Campus, and to IT gurus who have fixed computer threats when I began to imagine that the technology was taking over from the writing process.

Special mention for support over the years goes to my long-term co-author Emeritus Professor John Sugden; our three FIFA-related books in the late 1990s and the early 2000s set the scene for a form of investigative research that has informed overall understanding of the history, sociology and politics of the FIFA story.

On the domestic front, once again I must express unlimited gratitude for the support of Bernie Kirrane, Alys Tomlinson, Rowan Tomlinson, Jo Humphreys and Sinead Kirrane, a quintet of gems.

1
INTRODUCTION: FIFA – WHAT'S AT STAKE?

Football, widely perceived as the most popular team sport on earth, is ruled over by the world governing body FIFA (the Fédération Internationale de Football Association). Formed in 1904 in Paris by a small group of enthusiasts representing seven European nations, FIFA has evolved into one of the world's most powerful and high-profile sporting governing bodies, with 211 member associations under its control, and global media audiences of several billion for its prime spectacle, the men's World Cup. Yet despite its achievements, FIFA has generated controversies and criticism as much as accolades and respect. Its expanding networks of football administrators across the world have, for instance, included individuals who have neglected their responsibilities and seriously undermined FIFA's core values.

In FIFA's overall narrative it is revealing to track power dynamics across the phases that have led the organization to where it is now. I first began writing on FIFA in the mid-1980s, a decade or so after television and opportunistic corporations had begun to bring big money into the game on an international scale. Only a few journalists were then interested in what this small outfit on the banks of Lake Zurich was up to. But the profile of the (men's) World Cup competition was growing, and FIFA was selling advertising space to the highest bidder and eagerly granting broadcasting rights, thereby filling the organization's coffers. Along with the International Olympic Committee (IOC), FIFA was revolutionizing the global sport economy; football was emerging as one of the world's most prominent cultural commodities.

What, then, is at stake in exploring, understanding and critiquing the past, present and future of FIFA? Football's global constituency – its followers, enthusiasts, participants at all levels – has more access to the elite game than could possibly have been imagined back in FIFA's Paris office in 1904. Leagues and competitions have been established in countries and territories worldwide, and in recent decades the profile of the women's game has become stronger season by season. At the same time, football has become a money-led international business, framed at its highest levels as an irresistible spectacle generating cycle after cycle of excitement and drama for ever-larger audiences. The grassroots, from which of course footballers emerge, have become increasingly sidelined. Generations of football enthusiasts in local communities have experienced the pain of disconnection from their traditional club as more and more money has poured into the sport. Players who may have lived just down the road from fans have become less and less accessible as they have moved up the social ladder; the cost of a ticket has escalated as clubs have sought to survive; the connections of clubs and players with local communities have dwindled; and the power of media sponsors has distorted the patterns of attendance. The trajectory of the potential professional footballer has launched him – and more recently her – into a global soccerspace far removed from the local communities and grassroots in which the game first flourished.

What is at stake is not yet clear enough – but as the game has expanded, catapulting FIFA into the global consciousness, for many something has been lost. The global spectacle on our screens does little for community relations and collective identities, or overlooked issues such as race, gender and inequality. In this book I recognize the scale of FIFA's achievements but also highlight, alongside the oversights, cases of collaboration, collusion, corruption and criminality within the governing body and its affiliated organizations. Maybe we should recognize that what FIFA is actually for is the football enthusiasts themselves, the fans and the followers. The fans are the lifeblood of the football body – locally, regionally, nationally. I was reminded of this in an *Observer* piece by Alexandra Topping, in which she described in January 2025 preparing to take one of her children with her to see Premier League sides Everton and Bournemouth at the former's Goodison Park ground (Liverpool) in a round of the FA Cup, the world's oldest football competition. If Everton lost, the match would be the final FA Cup game to be held at the ground as the club moved the following season to its new £800 million stadium. It lost. But this was not the point. Topping elaborated on her lifelong commitment to this club, its location and its character, emphasizing that 'in the multibillion-dollar era of industrialised football – where fan eyeballs are units on a spreadsheet, where clubs are not passion projects but investment vehicles – the bones of a place still matter. History, memory and belonging still matter'.[1] So too do issues of equality, inclusivity and identity within those histories and memories.

So to answer the question 'What is FIFA for?' it is helpful to consider what FIFA really *is* and *should be* for. It has become pretty obvious in the modern phase of international football that the top national leagues and the most high-profile and lucrative cross-national competitions are anchored in more and more globally based deals with corporate sponsors, and then there are the parallel demands of the leading media 'partners' setting our screening schedules for us across the world. It struck me that in one sense we all know this, and somehow or other as we leave the stadium (if lucky enough to get in), the sports bar or local pub, or our own increasingly crammed screen schedule, there is very little to say – that's just the way it is, how the game's developed. But there *is* more to say than this, as costs of streaming services in the home and at public venues rise without consultation or debate, prices of season and match tickets rocket, and a culture of communication based in smartphones and online accounts atomizes the experience of consuming the spectacle.

Amorphous as it might be, it is the fan base, comprising generations of followers, which is in essence the core stakeholder in the football culture and 'product'. Without an audience there is no show. What then does FIFA really offer to its biggest stakeholder of all? Guardian of the game, with astonishing rising profile across the world, FIFA continues to claim credit for the unprecedented and seemingly inexorable expansion and development of professional football at all levels in every corner of the world. Is this what FIFA, the governing body of world football, is really for?

For answers, we need to step back, get a sense of the history of the game and develop an understanding of FIFA's evolving responsibilities and strategies, its successes and its failures. That's a big ask, but for the sake of football's extensive public and the future of the game it is surely a necessary task. This will take us to the icy shores of Greenland – population 56,000 – where the Football Association of Greenland (or, for the locals, KAK, the acronym of their native term) has been building a case to hop on to the FIFA pyramid, as the 42nd member of the Confederation of North, Central America and Caribbean Association Football (CONCACAF).[2] And, inevitably, to the biggest

CONCACAF member, the United States (population 340 million), where many of FIFA's activities have been focused in the 2020s. In particular, the quadrennial men's World Cup Final tournament will see the United States Soccer Federation (USSF), along with co-hosts Canada and Mexico, stage the expanded men's World Cup in summer 2026.

FIFA president Gianni Infantino wrote in his Foreword to the FIFA Forward Development Programme (Forward 3.0) in 2022, 'I look forward to continuing to work with everyone in the worldwide football community to develop the modern, accessible and inclusive global game that we envision'.[3] We will see in later chapters of this book what Infantino really meant by this. Whatever his priorities, the rationale for this book is the necessity, despite burgeoning studies of the FIFA phenomenon, for a short, accessible and comprehensive overview of the contributions of FIFA to our global sport culture. This is combined with an accompanying informed critical analysis of how FIFA got to where it is, asking at what price this has been achieved and how it has affected the organization's credibility and integrity.

Beyond the institutional practices built in to FIFA itself, the organization claims to speak for a worldwide constituency, comprising players at all levels and those who participate as spectators of the more elite level of the game – a global mass to which FIFA pays a form of lip-service in a conceit shared with its international partner, the IOC; the conceit is made up of references to and celebration of the FIFA or the IOC 'family'. But things are not so simple; cultural critic Theodor Adorno tells us that sports belong to 'the realm of unfreedom, no matter where they are organized'.[4] Whether you are a young casual footballer playing in the local park, a well-coached schoolkid with aspirations to get into the elite level of the game, a committed fan or follower with strong views on the significance of the game – all of these expressing themselves in their own chosen spaces and settings, their individual realms – FIFA's role as the voice and face of global football governance has enabled it to gain control of such realms, asserting its organizational power over football at all levels. Yet its often ruthless power plays are camouflaged by its long-established dominant position and constant reiteration of lofty principles.[5]

Therefore, to understand what FIFA is for we must consider who and what FIFA really is, and where and why it runs its operations as it does. A critical analysis of FIFA demands what the French sociologist Pierre Bourdieu, in an essay on the foundations of ethics, calls 'a politics of morality' based upon working constantly to unveil 'hidden differences between ... the limelight and the backrooms of political life', between 'official theory and actual practice'.[6]

The book, then, is organized to take readers on a worldwide journey through time and space, at the end of which they will be better able to answer the question that frames the project.[7] My primary aim is to illuminate the role of FIFA for football enthusiasts and readers whose interests include what goes on in the corridors of power away from the action on the pitch, and/or how abuses of power in football governance can be exposed and contested. Ideally, such readers will take away continuing questions on issues relating to the role of FIFA in the contemporary world. In responding to such issues and questions, and aided by critical interpretive perspectives that frame much of the discussion in *What Is FIFA For?*, the football fan and enthusiast can add his/her own voice to the debates that must be brought to bear on the world governing body's *modus operandi* in relation to its flawed, and sometimes fraudulent, governance of the world's most popular sport.

2
FIFA AND THE MAKING OF THE MODERN GAME

The development of modern football in the 19th century required the formalization of the sport with standardized rules which could be applied widely enough to enable the growth of the professional game at national and international levels. These processes established a shared legacy that enabled FIFA to be formed in Paris in 1904, presenting itself as the body that would represent the common interests of football across the world, despite the Eurocentric composition of the founding group.

The global profile of football and FIFA

Association football is widely acknowledged as the most popular participation and spectator sport in the world. FIFA itself, in its 'football landscape' overview in 2021, put the number of football fans and followers around the world at five billion,[1] over half the global population. Such a global profile has been created by the commodification of the game and the vast sums of money that have poured into football from multinationals and the marketing and media industries. The top levels of the men's game in particular have become enriched, and in the 2023–2024 season Spain's Real Madrid 'created football history', becoming 'the first football club to generate €1 billion [US$1.16 billion] across a single season'.[2] FIFA's quadrennial budget for the financial cycle 2023–2026 was an estimated US$11 billion. The level of money in the game is unprecedented, though unevenly distributed.

The roots of the game in pre-modern societies and civilizations bear virtually no resemblance to the contemporary spectacle. After all, little was needed to propel a round object around a designated space, using for the most part players' feet. There has nevertheless not been a lack of claimants for the title of originators of the game. Egyptian, Greek and Roman forms of ball games have all been identified, with Egypt in 2000 BC producing balls made of papyrus, wood and leather.[3] But it was China that the then FIFA president Sepp Blatter flattered with the label of originator of the ball-kicking game, 'announcing in 2005 that Linzi was the birthplace of world football some 2,000 years ago'.[4]

The previous year Blatter had spoken at the Beijing Football Expo, saying: 'We honour the Chinese people for their country's role as the cradle of the earliest forms of football, having firmly planted the roots of our sport and helping set the course for it to grow into the beautiful game that it is today.' FIFA's communications machine disseminated this event under the heading 'Football fever hits Beijing', and Blatter's address was greeted with the strong support of the Asian Football Confederation (AFC) and the Chinese Sports Ministry.[5] Blatter was referring to *cuju*, a form of ball game in which kicking was fundamental, though handling the ball and tackling opponents were to some extent permitted. Two teams played on a specified space, marked out with clear boundaries and goals at either end.

There is no doubt that kicking dominated the game. As observed by David Goldblatt, evidence suggests that *cuju* was played in the royal household of the Han dynasty (206 BCE–221 CE), among the military, and in successive imperial dynasties for several centuries, though its format was continually adapted to new technologies and trends. Goldblatt points too to numerous forms of ball play that have been identified in other cultures and civilizations, from Malaysia to Japan, among Aboriginal Australians and Native Americans. Goldblatt puts the origins debate to bed with the pithy comment that '[t]he sphere [ball] is as old as the world. Kicking is as old as humanity. The Ancients knew the ball, but football is born of modernity'.[6] Deep anthropological analysis, careful reflection and modesty have not, though, been characteristic of FIFA's public image; in the museum in China, in Shandong Province, images and pictures of the FIFA president, including a substantial bust, were installed and remain on show throughout the museum. Blatter's visit to China was essentially an attempt to boost interest in the sport across the country; the demise of the Chinese Super League and the fading fortunes of the Chinese national men's and women's teams suggest that Blatter's efforts had little long-term impact.

Origins of the modern game

Modern football began in early industrial Britain. Englishman Sir Stanley Rous wrote in 1974 – his last year as FIFA president – that an early form of football was outlawed by England's King Edward III in an edict of 1349; but that in the 'rough and tumble kind of football ... played in the towns and the countryside' of England's Middle Ages the only law which applied was apparently ' "[w]herever the ball goes, the mob goes" ... often a scene of riot and tumult, with accompanying disorder'.[7] Such a rough and unready form of street football would guarantee little standardization of the game. In Italy in 1580, Giovanni de' Bardi, Florentine patron of music and the arts as well as writer, composer and soldier, published a set of rules for the game of *calcio*. These appear to have had little influence in Britain, where Shakespeare's two acknowledgements of the game of football seemed to confirm the low esteem in which it was held.[8] Nevertheless, in 1680 some form of football did win royal patronage from King Charles II of England.[9]

The turning point for the modern form of football was, in England, the second half of the 19th century, when organized forms of the game were established, and the sport emerged as a coherent, codified cultural form engaging men across the class spectrum. Whatever shape or form the game was taking in the 19th century, there was an increasingly pressing need to establish a common playing code. Upper-class males in elite public schools – such as Harrow, Rugby, Eton, Westminster and Charterhouse – were playing the game according to their own distinctive, idiosyncratic principles. The Carthusian football enthusiasts of Charterhouse, raised to play their game in the seriously confined space of the cloisters of an old Carthusian monastery in London until 1872, prioritized 'dribbling' the ball;[10] Etonians favoured the high and the long kick; Rugbeians caught the ball and ran with it, thus gifting the school's name to the Rugby Football Union variant that would, in 1871, split with the hegemonic Association Football code.[11]

Arriving, as many of them did, at one of the dominant elitist institutions of Oxford or Cambridge University, these public schoolboys found that clashes of style and interpretations of imprecise rules produced chaos on the playing fields. Such young men were also anchored in individual colleges of the university, so that inter-collegiate as well as inter-university fixtures could be undermined by the lack of a shared understanding of how the game should be played. Competing models were championed for several decades from the 1840s onwards; in 1846 Rugby School wrote down the rules of the game for the first time, and two years later alumni from the University of Cambridge proposed a shared view of its fundamentals as a basis for a common code.

These were not widely accepted though, as young men who had played their football at other public schools simply stuck, out of loyalty and convenience, to their own school's code, written or not, but engraved in the cultural legacies of their *alma mater*.

Nevertheless, the game had its adherents, and supportive commentators were not slow to praise what they saw as its core qualities. Author and critic Melvyn Bragg quotes a passage from the *Labour Force Survey Quality Review* of 1863:

> [T]he fascination of this gentle pastime is its mimic war, and it is waged with the individual prowess of the Homeric conflicts. ... The play is played out by boys with that dogged determination to win, that endurance of pain, that bravery of combative spirit, by which the adult is trained to face the cannon-ball with equal alacrity.[12]

And this date, 1863, marks without doubt the intervention that made all the difference in the genealogy of the game. It was on 26 October 1863 that representatives of 11 London clubs and schools met at the Freemason's Tavern in central London, in the heart of the lawyerly area of Lincoln's Inn Fields. Here the decision was taken to establish the world's first national 'Football Association' (*the* FA, as then emphasized, and argued for to this day), and at a meeting in the same place a couple of months later they approved the list of 14 rules that would shape the game. It was not by any measure a smooth process to get all participants to adopt these rules and initially just 18 clubs joined the new FA, the other clubs simply carrying on as before. The Sheffield club, with a middle-class leadership and a working-class membership, already had its own rules, though was from the start an active member of the FA and influential in identifying some updates to the rules, integrating them with the FA's in 1877.

The upper-class grip on the story of the emergence of modern football has been loosened by scholarly interventions that remind us that an industrializing Britain generated towns, businesses and cities with expanding populations which were looking to add activities to their non-work lives. As the 19th century progressed, there was popular protest at the lack of quality living conditions and forms of leisure for the population as a whole, for the people. Schools and churches were run by football enthusiasts – 'soccer's missing men', as J.A. Mangan and Colm Hickey have called them. Their research has identified how teachers in elementary schools made influential contributions to the growth of adult football, 'through the founding and furthering of many of the major clubs that we know today, as in the Midlands ... where Wolverhampton Wanderers, Aston Villa, Northampton, Walsall and Stoke amongst others had links with schoolteachers'.[13] Other similarly insightful work has questioned the accuracy of the account, attributing the overall growth of the modern form of the game to the public schoolboys and university elites; in his book *Football: The First Hundred Years – the Untold Story*, Adrian Harvey identifies the profiles and origins of 93 clubs in the years 1830–1859, showing that in England 'during the 1840s the North was the heartland of football, far surpassing the South. In the 1850s the situation was somewhat reversed, with the South taking the lead'.[14] More generally, as observed by sociologist Richard Giulianotti, between 1830 and 1860 'a huge vacuum had appeared in popular leisure', with the disappearance of 'old bucolic pastimes like bear-baiting, cock-fighting and village folk-football ... as the general populace moved into the towns for work'.[15]

Harvey also examines the social composition of teams, confirming that School was just one influencing factor of five categories, the others being Local, Clubs, Military and Occupations.[16] His passionate analysis concludes with the conviction – convincingly presented – that association football in England was 'created by a mixture of influences, stemming from both inside and outside the walls of the public schools'.[17] Whatever this mixture looked like, three prominent factors clearly drove the development of the game.[18]

First, the FA fizzed into life, bringing different perspectives together in integrating initiatives; FA secretary Charles Alcock was the man of the moment, tidying up laws, even organizing a match to demonstrate the revisions. Second, new generations of football players, men who needed reliable and adequately paid jobs, preferred the association football model to the still rough and relatively wild game of rugby that could so often lead to injury. And third, Alcock's initiative in setting up competitive cup football, with the first FA Challenge Cup Competition Final in 1871, laid the foundation for the popularization of the game among the working classes, who were to challenge and then supersede the public school teams. The symbolic moment for this transfer of status, power and prestige was the visit of Blackburn Olympic, a team of Lancashire working men, to London, where they defeated Old Etonians in the 1883 Cup Final. Since then, no southern amateur side has ever won the FA Cup. The Blackburn players, funded by a local manufacturer, prepared in Blackpool – for their semi-final as well as the final – with a full week's training before the games. A mere two years later, faced with the organized opposition of increasing numbers of para-professional players and owners, Alcock saw the future; rule changes were made in 1884 and professional status was formally legalized in England by the FA in 1885. The FA therefore could retain the responsibility for controlling the emerging football world and in 1888 the Football League was formed, going on to establish 'the commercial face of professional football'.[19] The social class pendulum was swinging towards the people.

Also vital to the growth of the game was an internationalist perspective among those who were looking to support a shared governance model across countries with varying cultures, traditions and languages. Domestically – within the single nation state of Great Britain – the (English) FA was created in 1863, the Scottish Football Association in 1873, the Football Association of Wales in 1876 and the Irish Football Association in 1880. In 1872

England and Scotland played their first official international match in a goalless draw at the West of Scotland Cricket Club, Partick; the Scotland side comprised solely Queen's Park players, as the Scottish football association was not yet formed.[20] The four bodies joined together to agree a uniform code for international matches – for instance, to replace a pragmatic yet absurd tendency to switch rules after half-time in international matches – and in 1886 formally established the International Football Association Board (IFAB), which, in the words of FIFA president Dr João Havelange a century later, 'created a competent body, solely responsible over all these [100] years, for the international standardization, supplementation and modification of the Laws of the Game. And that was how international match competition began'.[21] South American and European national sides appeared on the scene – Austria, Hungary, Argentina and Uruguay – in 1902; and 'Belgium and France in 1904, a month before the formation of FIFA'.[22]

The IFAB itself, allying itself more formally with FIFA in recent years, is an irreplaceable institution that has ensured the longevity of football in the latter's sustainable and seemingly unstoppable climb to the highest echelons of global popular culture. And that means not just play or exercise – it is via such modest-looking initiatives of the time as the IFAB that football culture(s) have survived and thrived, to the point of entry into the world(s) of money, spectacle and consumption on a global scale.

Beginnings, tensions, trajectories

The developments in England stimulated the more widespread adoption of the game across the European continent, but also in more distant countries via the presence and influence of British professionals, industrialists, educators, missionaries and the military; at least one initiative on the international front occurred prior to the attempts to codify the game in Britain.[23] In Australia a club was created in Melbourne in 1858 playing on the basis of rules very like those to be approved by the FA in 1863. Elsewhere, Buenos Aires Football Club was formed by Britons in 1865. British soldiers in Montreal, Canada, played matches according to the Eton College code in 1862 and 1866. In Bangalore, India, British army officers from different regiments played each other, adhering to the rules of Harrow. In France, English businessmen living in Paris created the Bois de Boulogne Football and Athletics Club in 1863. Influenced possibly by Thomas Hughes's Rugby School-inspired novel, *Tom Brown's Schooldays*, the Oneida Football Club was founded in Boston in 1862. The stage was set for a surge of development that would make football perhaps one of the most lucrative cross-cultural initiatives of all time. But initially, international leadership did not emerge from an English base. The FA in London showed scant interest in the creation of a world governing body, despite polite overtures from European pioneers.

It was in France, then, in May 1904, that seven European nations set up FIFA at a meeting in Paris, creating an international organization initially run by a bunch of young, male, white, European volunteers who would be succeeded for decades by a tiny staff with limited resources. The meeting was initiated by the French and hosted in a back room of the modest headquarters of the USFSA (Union des sociétés françaises de sports athlétiques) at 229 Rue Saint-Honoré in the classy 1st *arrondissement*. Robert Guérin, sport journalist and secretary of the football committee of the USFSA, represented France along with representatives from Belgium, Denmark, Netherlands, Spain, Sweden and Switzerland. Guérin accepted the role of founding FIFA president, football administrator Louis Muhlinghaus of Belgium took on the task of general secretary and treasurer, assisted by football organizer and former post/mail inspector Ludwig Sylow of Denmark. Carl Hirschman (Netherlands) and Viktor Schneider (Switzerland) were made vice-presidents. Spain's representative was USFSA secretary André Espir, asked by the Madrid Football Club (later renamed Real Madrid) to represent the interests of his country (the Royal Spanish Football Federation was not created until 1913). Sweden was there by proxy, getting Denmark's Sylow to represent its interests. Germany's Deutscher Fußball Bund (DFB), founded in Leipzig in 1873, had been involved in framing initial statutes for the new organization and picked a veteran member, Gustav Manning, to attend the Paris meeting; but he missed his cross-Channel ferry from England to France. A hastily organized replacement couldn't get there on time either. So the German DFB sent a telegram committing to the formation of what was to become FIFA, and thereafter laid the rather unconvincing claim to be the first football association to officially join.[24]

Committee members of the new organization and their successors over the coming decades claimed expenses but drew no salaries. Whatever the odds, FIFA kept in the game, and cannot be underestimated for its resilience, commitment and continuity. The British associations were soon to join, and on Guérin's resignation in 1906 Englishman Daniel Woolfall became president. Membership expanded beyond Europe with applications from South Africa and the Americas approved prior to the First World War. FIFA barely survived the international enmity of the war years, and when Woolfall died the month before the end of hostilities Carl Hirschman, general secretary from 1906 to 1931, stepped in as acting/interim president and operated out of his offices in Amsterdam to revive the organization. As a banker, he offered some financial stability to FIFA but lost its assets when his own stock trading company went bankrupt in the financial crash of 1929. Jules Rimet had assumed the leadership role in 1921 and presided over periods of relatively steady growth and development before and after the Second World War, including, most significantly, the introduction of the World Cup in 1930 and a move to new headquarters in Zurich, Switzerland, in 1932. He led FIFA through to 1951, and was succeeded by three more presidents until 1974, when the baton was passed by Sir Stanley Rous to Dr João Havelange, ushering

> **Box 2.1: What was this institutional newcomer FIFA all about?**
>
> The essential goal of the pioneering international sports organization was to conduct sports on an international basis. This might have been driven by the imperatives of imperial domination – as in the case of Great Britain and its empire and later commonwealth – or for national self-aggrandizement through sporting prowess – as with newer unified nations flexing their muscles against longer-established nation states. Whatever the specific case, though, rules had to be commonly understood, competitions organized in coherent and reproducible fashion, and diplomatic barriers overcome in an ethos of common cause and co-operation.[25]

in a dramatically transformational phase of expansion and marketization.

The structures of accountability have looked inadequate or close to non-existent from FIFA's beginnings, as we shall see throughout this book. For over 120 years it has, excluding interim/acting stand-ins, had just nine presidents. The combination of rarely accountable leaders holding on to power alongside fragile principles vaguely sustaining the organizational infrastructure of the governing body have proved destabilizing throughout FIFA's history.

The nine FIFA presidents from 1904 to the mid-2020s have all been men, all white, and nearly all European:

Table 2.1: **FIFA's first nine presidents**

Name, nationality and former career	Tenure
Robert Guérin (France, journalist)	1904–1906
Daniel Burley Woolfall (England, civil servant)	1906–1918
Jules Rimet (France, lawyer)	1921–1954
Rodolphe William Seeldrayers (Belgium, lawyer)	1954–1955
Arthur Drewry (England, fish merchant)	1955–1961
Sir Stanley Rous (England, schoolmaster, international referee)	1961–1974
Dr João Havelange (Brazil, lawyer, businessman and Olympic athlete)	1974–1998
Joseph Sepp Blatter (Switzerland, marketing executive)	1998–2015
Gianni Infantino (Switzerland, law background, sport administration)	2016–present

The sole non-European figure, the Brazilian lawyer and entrepreneur João Havelange – holder of the second-longest presidency – 24 years, behind Jules Rimet's tenure of 33 years – breaches the dominance of the four Western European countries.

FIFA developed slowly but doggedly, staging its inaugural world championship in 1930, more than a quarter of a century after its formation; by then it had dealt with difficult disputes over the rules and organization of the game, and its membership continued to grow, boosted in 1910 at its Milan Congress by 'the admittance, against the Statutes, of Scotland, Ireland and Wales' (allowed membership even though they were not independent nation states); enabling national teams to participate at the 1912 Stockholm Olympic Games, a first step 'along the road which would lead to the total control of the world football tournament'; and welcoming 40 members to the first post-war Congress in Geneva in 1923.[26] It was already the world's largest sporting federation, despite its origins as a small voluntary group, 'a privileged gentleman's club with no headquarters and no jurisdiction over either the laws of the game or the competitions themselves'.[27] FIFA was nevertheless able to establish and retain control over the development of the game because the national football associations (NFAs) accepted its authority and, once it moved to Zurich and was reconstituted under the Swiss Civil Code in 1932, the permissive nature of Swiss law meant that its decisions were unlikely to be legally challenged.

FIFA revised and rewrote its statutes after the Second World War and had established and reorganized regional confederations by the 1960s, against the will of the former French president Jules Rimet. It was led by Englishman Sir Stanley Rous from 1961 to 1974, who lived on his pension and FIFA expenses. He expedited FIFA's modernization and international expansion, transcending the parochial Eurocentrism of Rimet, by travelling the world promoting the game, establishing coaching expertise and refereeing capacity across the world and turning the presidency into a globally significant role.[28] Rous did, though, ignore FIFA's commercial potential because of his lifelong voluntarist principles, and this, along with his stubbornly accommodating stance on the issue of apartheid in South Africa, opened the gates for a non-, one might also say anti-, European candidate.

Dr. João Havelange was to change the profile and scale of ambitions of the world governing body.

In 1996, I asked Havelange about the nature of his achievements over the last quarter of a century; he confirmed somewhat immodestly that he had delivered all that he promised in his campaign for the presidency, concluding with the observation that much of this was down to his skill in applying industry principles to football business, and that consequently through his unprecedented actions 'the FIFA administration service may be considered perfect'.[29] Such a claim would be undermined by the exposure of the true nature of the adminstrations of Havelange and his protégé and successor Blatter. An overview of the background to the 2015 crisis demonstrates the scale of the reputational

Figure 2.1: Sepp Blatter, general secretary of FIFA, and João Havelange, president of FIFA, holding the Adidas Tango España, 1982

damage that accumulated throughout the Havelange and Blatter regimes.

Reputational catastrophe

FIFA's major asset is the men's World Cup, and the bidding processes to win the hosting rights for the finals tournament have repeatedly generated controversy. The choice in 2010 of Qatar as 2022 host has been described as 'the most corrupt World Cup bidding contest in history', a deal in part brokered by Mohamed bin Hammam, a billionaire Qatari businessman.[30] He had been a long-standing member of the FIFA and AFC executive committees (ExCos), and AFC president from 2002. Bin Hammam had funded Blatter's successful 1998 presidential campaign, but subsequently been alienated by Blatter, who failed to support the Qatari's bid for the FIFA presidency in 2007. Nevertheless, he was able to promote Qatar's image for its successful World Cup bid by, for example, staging events and supporting the African Confederation in a high-profile Congress.

After the Qatar decision, bin Hammam used Jack Warner, president of the Confederation of North, Central America and Caribbean Association Football (CONCACAF), to persuade the Caribbean Football Union's officials to support his bid for the presidency in 2011 by handing envelopes containing US$40,000 to each of its national representatives in a hotel room at a Caribbean Football Union conference in Port of Spain. They were told, on bin Hammam's behalf, that the officials had distributed the money so that no one should feel that 'anybody has any obligation for your vote because of what gift you have given them'.[31] Significantly, the money had been sent via bank accounts in New York City and on to another US account shortly after the scheme had been uncovered and Warner had resigned. These transfers enabled the FBI and US Department of Justice (DoJ) to intervene.

Chuck Blazer, the CONCACAF general secretary, alerted Blatter to the plot, so bin Hammam withdrew his candidacy, was suspended by FIFA, and resigned from the AFC; Blatter was re-elected in June 2011. The scandals continued, as did the exposés by investigative journalists and academics. In 2012, alerted by Andrew Jennings' earlier revelations, the FBI/Internal Revenue Service Criminal Investigation Department pressurized Blazer to wear a wire in the committee rooms and hotel lobbies of FIFA representatives at the London 2012 Summer Olympics, and worked with the DoJ to amass the evidence that precipitated the 2015 crisis.[32] At the end of the following year, in a sealed court in Brooklyn, New York, Blazer himself faced a number of charges relating to corruption, 'to events involving an exchange of elicit payments for one purpose or another', identifying 'FIFA and its attendant or related constituent organization as what we call an enterprise, a RICO enterprise', a 'Racketeering Influenced Corrupt Organization'. 'Conspiracy' was the foremost charge in the proceedings, alleging 'a conspiracy to corrupt this enterprise through the anticipated payment of funds pursuant to various criminal schemes. ... A conspiracy to use wire transfers to effect the payment of monies'.[33] FIFA's reputation was in tatters.

Once perceived as a 'master of meetings ... a figure of charismatic authority whom few crossed',[34] the veteran Havelange resigned from his honorary presidency of FIFA 11 days before the FIFA Adjudicatory Committee report in April 2013 reprimanded him, his son-in-law, and top Confederación Sudamericana de Fútbol (CONMEBOL) official Nicolás Leoz, for receiving huge 'bribes' (though not recognized as such under Swiss law) from marketing giant International Sport and Leisure (ISL) between 1992 and 2000, when Blatter had been general secretary and then president. Blatter himself could not, though, be directly implicated and Hans-Joachim Eckert, chair of the FIFA Ethics Committee's Adjudicatory Chamber, merely described Blatter's conduct as 'clumsy'.[35] Global protest against FIFA and its leadership was intensifying, from its Swiss base to the beaches of Brazil.

Figure 2.2: Protest on Copacabana Beach, 10 June 2014, Brazil men's World Cup

This confirmed the looseness and embedded hypocrisy of FIFA's internal processes and inter-organizational practices. In 2014 at the men's World Cup Finals in Brazil the FIFA president Sepp Blatter was already a target for activists, critics and journalists. The previous year had seen him derided and publicly shamed by protesters for whom the Confederations Cup, won by Brazil in a 3–0 triumph over Spain, was a symbol of excess, inequality and the abuse of power as the crises and cases of corruption multiplied. But on the eve of the World Cup, in May 2014, a film premiered at the Cannes Festival in the South of France. FIFA splashed out a reported US$22.2 million (of a total budget of US$26.1 million) on *United Passions: The True Story of the World Cup* (see Box 2.2), which further undermined the governing body's reputation and credibility.[36] *Guardian* writer Jordan Hoffman's pithy review stated that 'FIFA propaganda is pure cinematic excrement', though noted that the film could serve as a 'valuable case study' of 'proof of corporate insanity'.[37]

Blatter was even re-elected after the Zurich arrests of 2015, promising increased income to the NFAs and turning a blind eye to corruption in local associations unless it threatened his own position. He also claimed that such corrupt practices were not FIFA's responsibility but, for instance, had been organized by the four indicted CONCACAF presidents who had already been banned by the ethics committee he had himself set up back in 2003/ 2004. These four, from Trinidad and Tobago, Honduras, Cayman Islands, and Barbados added up to quite a rogues' gallery of corrupt presidents from a single confederation.[38]

Box 2.2: FIFA goes to Hollywood

United Passions tells the story of the creation of FIFA in 1904 and its development of the men's World Cup from 1930 to 2010, the year South Africa hosted it (providing the opportunity to include shots of Nelson Mandela celebrating the event, won by Spain). The movie was trailed as the story of impassioned, young football enthusiasts uniting to create a body – FIFA – that then went on to create the first World Cup. Alongside Gérard Depardieu, who played the role of Jules Rimet, were Tim Roth, playing Joseph 'Sepp' Blatter, and Sam Neill as João Havelange. Sam Neill told the German magazine *Der Spiegel* that he only took part because he needed the money, declaring in his autobiography that he didn't care at all about soccer. Neither it seems did the movie-goers of Phoenix, Arizona, where the film grossed US$9 in its opening weekend, the price of a single ticket. Takings for this box-office bomb were tiny; on release in the United States, the film grossed just short of US$700. The focus is upon the vicissitudes of Jules Rimet's two and a half decades at the presidential helm; the last days of Sir Stanley Rous, portrayed as a spiteful loser to the first non-European FIFA president Havelange; and the latter's topsy-turvy relationship with his new Number Two and successor Blatter.

And, further damnation via Wikipedia and YouTube: prior to release, comedian John Oliver lampooned the film in a segment on his show *Last Week Tonight*, saying that the 'movie, like FIFA itself, looks terrible' and asking, 'Who makes a sports film where the heroes are the executives?'

Blatter and others were therefore initially able to avoid the worst consequences of the 2015 crisis, but the accumulated crises, ethical breaches and most of all the US intervention without doubt exposed the embedded malpractices of a corrupt generation of FIFA personnel; subjected the organization to intense criticism from its stakeholders; and forced the FIFA leadership to initiate further internal reforms with promised long-term consequences.

The 2015 corruption crisis

The indictment that created the most dramatic crisis in FIFA's history targeted FIFA officials who held such positions 'by operation of the FIFA statutes, as well as officials of one or more other bodies'.[39] The first batch of 14 indicted defendants – a further indictment would come later in December of the same year, identifying another 16 individuals – generated three categories: soccer officials involved in financial matters and deals within FIFA and one of its 'constituent organizations'; company executives in sport media and marketing bodies; and bankers, businessmen and 'trusted intermediaries' laundering illicit payments. Nine of the defendants in the 20 May indictment and named in the 27 May press release were in the first category of FIFA official; four were sport marketing executives; and just one fitted the third category, working in the broadcasting business but operating as an intermediary to facilitate illicit payments.

The first two categories of corruption and criminality identified by the DoJ were refined by FIFA conspirators over a period of a quarter of a century, and allowed the culprits to rise to 'positions of power and influence' across the world of football. Networks of marketing companies dealt with the governing bodies of football, gaining control over 'regions and localities throughout the world ... increasingly intertwined with one another and with the sports marketing companies that enabled them to generate unprecedented profits', in particular through the sale of media rights to matches and competitions. FIFA and the crooked individuals, or conspirators, in its system were seen by the US authorities as a form of enterprise operating on a global scale, milking the system and effectively operating as a successful 'racketeering conspiracy'.[40] The indictments were framed by the DoJ's application of the Racketeer Influenced and Corrupt Organizations Act, a US federal law passed in 1970, geared to taking action against ongoing criminal organizations. The DoJ constructed a 'FIFAgraph' (see Figure 2.3) to demonstrate the global reach of the FIFA criminal enterprise, and the prominence of the two continental confederations (CCs) covering the Americas and the Caribbean.

The origins of such a conspiracy that operated for so long and on such a massive scale are considered in more detail in Chapter 4. As for the final years of Blatter's presidency, from the Qatar decision of 2010 onwards, they can only be seen as a form of implosion

Figure 2.3: The US Department of Justice's FIFAgraph – 'the Enterprise'

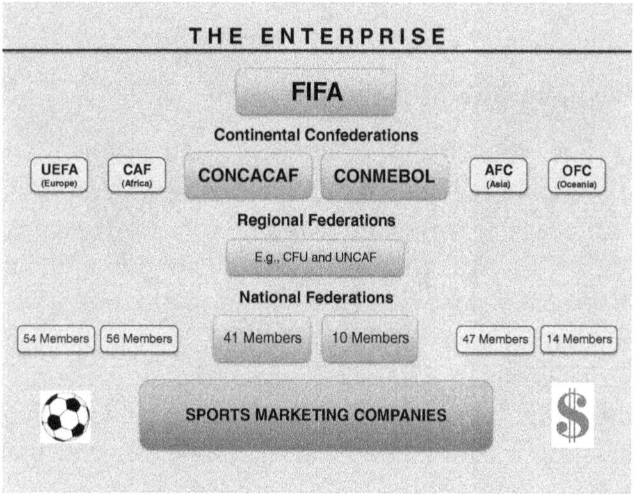

```
                        THE ENTERPRISE
                              FIFA
                      Continental Confederations
   UEFA     CAF    CONCACAF    CONMEBOL      AFC      OFC
  (Europe) (Africa)                         (Asia)  (Oceania)
                        Regional Federations
                         E.g., CFU and UNCAF
                         National Federations
  54 Members  56 Members  41 Members  10 Members  47 Members  14 Members

              SPORTS MARKETING COMPANIES
```

of the governing body as scandals continued and suspensions and bans were issued to more and more FIFA committee members who were exploiting their positions of responsibility in FIFA itself or affiliated networks. The imperious Havelange died aged 100 the year after the corruption crisis, but his 'legacy became tainted late in his life when details emerged of his complicity in a $100m bribery scandal that engulfed world football's governing body'.[41] The Havelange/Blatter dynasty had been crumbling for some time. For several years at least FIFA was seen as a byword for corruption, its credibility at its most fragile and its image permanently tarnished. It would hover on the edge of total catastrophe, threatened by continuing conflicts of interest and power plays within the organization.

The new broom

In early 2016 Gianni Infantino saw an opening in the race to replace Blatter. Following revelations of dubious, privately conducted financial transactions with his long-term ally Michel Platini, Blatter had little option but to resign his position. Infantino, then general secretary at the Union of European Football Associations (UEFA), adopted the core strategy of the former president: flatter the NFA representatives, promise them more and more money to fund their associations, remind them that FIFA's money is *their* money (and there will be much more of it in this new presidential cycle), and go forward in a spirit of revival and the promise of reform. Infantino offered a voice of the future, drawing too on his membership of the reform group established in late 2015. His rise to the FIFA presidency was cannily executed. Born in Brig, Switzerland, his Italian immigrant parentage gives him citizenship of both countries. His first languages are French, German and Italian, and in addition he speaks Arabic, English, Portuguese and Spanish. With such a linguistic range he is well-prepared to represent the global interests of world football. At the University of Fribourg he studied law, going on to work in sport-based organizations including UEFA, where he rose rapidly to the top leadership position.

We shall see in later chapters how the Infantino promises and practices have worked out. Meanwhile, in Chapter 3 we take a closer look at FIFA's organizational infrastructure, in the context of its core members, the 211 national associations and the six CCs, pointing to both its strengths and its weaknesses.

3
FIFA AND ITS MEMBERS

Globally, FIFA is made up of national football associations (NFAs) and continental confederations (CCs), two of which also include regional confederations. FIFA itself, a not-for-profit organization, oversees the global game and holds quadrennial Congresses attended by representatives of all NFAs and the CCs. It stages the men's and the women's World Cup tournaments; a revamped men's Club World Cup (CWC) (and, for women, an inaugural edition in 2028); and numerous tournaments for younger international teams. It also assumes responsibility for running the football tournaments at the Olympics. FIFA operates according to its own statutes and has in place an ethics committee that can investigate malpractice in the administration of the professional game.

Throughout its developmental phases, FIFA attracted an increasingly wide range of members from across the world, and in the mid-20th century the need for more regionalized forms of administration was recognized, leading to the setting up of FIFA-affiliated bodies representing different regions and continents. Veteran FIFA observer Keir Radnege believes, though, that such developments confused the essential simplicity of the NFAs and their relationship to FIFA. Looking back at the formation of FIFA, he reflects that 'the emergent patchwork of nation states certainly suited the ambition of fledgling FIFA. ... Borders meant national associations and national associations meant national teams'.[1] But, Radnege adds, 'as national team football generates millions of dollars hand-in-hand with fixture inflation, so the original concept is devalued'. National teams, initially established as vehicles for patriotism, went on to play in competitions that both FIFA and its CCs have turned into lucrative national and international spectacles focused primarily upon cash generation. In this process of expansion, and against some of the core principles of neutrality at the heart of the FIFA statutes, geopolitics and the commodification of spectacle have become inextricably linked to the game's development worldwide.

FIFA's members

In 2025 FIFA membership consisted of the 211 NFAs, outnumbering the member states of the United Nations (193), as FIFA grants membership to territories such as Gibraltar, welcomed into FIFA as its 211th NFA in 2016, though not a sovereign state. The NFAs also belong to a designated continental or regional confederation. Five of the six CCs were formed in the period 1954–1966, in a way emulating the model the

South American teams established with Confederación Sudamericana de Fútbol (CONMEBOL) in 1916. To date CONMEBOL has just ten members, sustaining its profile on the basis of South America's continuing prominence in the game, challenging the Eurocentric status of FIFA in a long-running rivalry between the South Americans and the Europeans that has dominated FIFA politics over the ensuing decades. This rivalry fuelled the initiative to establish UEFA (Union of European Football Associations) in 1954.

The Asian Football Confederation (AFC), also formed in 1954, now has 46 members split into five geographical sub-regions. Confédération Africaine de Football (CAF), established in 1957, also has five regional federations with 54 members in total. The giants of North and Central America – the United States, Canada and Mexico – gave the Confederation of North, Central America and Caribbean Association Football (CONCACAF) credibility and clout from its creation in 1961; drawing on the central American and Caribbean NFAs, the confederation had risen to 35 members by the time of the 2026 men's World Cup, hosted by the CC's giants. Sub-groups of CONCACAF were also established: the Caribbean Football Union, recommended by former FIFA president Rous, was inaugurated as a regional body in 1978; the Unión Centroamericana de Fútbol was founded in 1990. The last of the six CCs to be set up was the Oceania Football Confederation, formed in 1966 and numbering 11 members.

A membership of 211 is an extraordinary number of associations for FIFA to approve, monitor and, albeit in a distant and often remote sense, manage. Access to such a membership nevertheless offers FIFA the means to demonstrate the international scale of the professional game. In its 2021 annual report, FIFA announced the launch of the Professional Football Landscape, 'the first-ever digital database comprising key facts on players, clubs, transfers and top-tier competitions across all 211 member associations'.[2] It prefaced its 'takeaways' with a reminder that 'FIFA has an unwavering commitment to look after football's most important protagonists – the players', and ensured that throughout 2021 'further steps were taken to ensure the well-being and continued development of all players within the professional game'. The report added that the 'FIFA Professional Football Landscape was created for the *whole football community* [my italics] in order to monitor the professionalisation of football, in line with FIFA's strategic objective of mapping and promoting football development around the world in order to make the game truly global'. The primary takeaway revealed that 'nearly 130,000 professional players and more than 4,400 professional clubs have been identified around the world'. It wasn't too clear what the term 'professional' actually meant, or how different NFAs understood the term. Men's and women's football were both covered though in the responses of the member associations. But the notion of a 'whole football community' remains somewhat vague in relation to 'the professionalisation of football'.

FIFA's statutes allow each country/NFA a single vote on any issue at the FIFA Congress, which sounds like the purest form of democratic participation. This has not been, though, how FIFA works. Confederations have power when their NFAs vote together, representing regional interests and in some cases power blocs, as can be seen when candidates for the FIFA presidency are contesting the election, often with the support of a particular CC.

The five confederations formed between 1954 and 1966 were seen by future FIFA president Sir Stanley Rous as a means to achieve fair distribution of development resources and funds. Some FIFA observers – and advisers – have suggested that the confederations have not met the expectations of those who have so strongly backed them, but Rous was committed to completing what he saw as the perfect way to establish a worldwide profile for the game and educate players and referees in football's development in all corners of the planet. His long-term assistant/secretary Rose-Marie Breitenstein, who worked with him from 1961 until his death in 1986, recalls the passion with which he set about realizing this vision, but also recollects the number of problems that he had as FIFA president in his dealings with the 'South Americans'. She was referring here to CONMEBOL's belief in its own importance right from the date of its formation, tinged with its hostility towards a European-dominated FIFA:

> There were always people who were jealous of him, and maybe some South Americans, people who didn't know him, you know ... the South Americans were under this

impression because of former Presidents who had been European and British ... but the power was in Europe and in Great Britain and I think that this is what they were against in those days. ... I have been to Congresses of the South American Confederation and it was this power struggle with the South Americans against the Europeans.[3]

The power struggle that Breitenstein identified saw the Brazilian João Havelange, strongly backed by his small, tight and determined group of fellow South Americans in CONMEBOL, mount a challenge for the FIFA presidency in 1974. He could mobilize NFA votes to back his campaign in precisely the way Breitenstein foresaw: represent the Brits and the Europeans as the elite, make the case for a fairer democratic model, and – perhaps Havelange's trump card – draw the wider new electorate, in particular the African and Asian confederations, in to the bigger picture, whatever the price – a favour here, a bribe or two there – of a vote in the election itself. FIFA's NFA members and affiliated CCs were becoming more explicitly political in the game of global football governance.

Joining FIFA: 211 and counting

CONCACAF proudly says: 'As the governing body for football in North, Central America and the Caribbean the priority of Concacaf is to serve its 41 Member Associations, ensuring that we are delivering on our ... strategic goals.'[4] It thanks FIFA's Member Associations Division for providing crucial assistance and advice in areas 'that are instrumental to support the growth of our sport', emphasizing that 'the needs of the game across the region' do demand 'a close understanding'. FIFA itself highlights its 'focus', confirming its aim to support the 211 NFAs as well as the six confederations 'in the development, governance and administration of football'.[5] The Division also contributes to the implementation of FIFA Forward, 'a 360-degree tailor-made funding programme for our member associations with increased investment, impact and oversight'. Such declarations of commitment and support prove attractive to small NFAs, though of CONCACAF's 41 'members' six are not full members of FIFA. (Bonaire, French Guiana, Guadeloupe, Martinique, Saint Martin and Sint Maarten constitute a line-up of post-imperial French and Dutch territories and overseas collectivities.)

FIFA does support ongoing analysis of the performance levels of its members in its FIFA/Coca-Cola World Ranking system, reporting most recently a rise in performance by the minnows of the global game. This is one aspect of what FIFA really *could* be for: to provide genuine forms of funding and expertise to grow the game across the world, echoing the serious and authentic commitment of FIFA pioneers, particularly in the post-colonial period after the Second World War. Current FIFA president Gianni Infantino is well-known for his frequent meetings with political leaders across the world but in 2023 Infantino also visited Vanuatu, talking with NFA officials and the country's prime minister, and highlighting a need for further collaboration between

FIFA, the Oceanic Football Confederation, the Vanuatu Football Federation and the country's government: 'We will invest together, we will work together ... we will build because we want to give opportunities and chances for all children, all girls and all boys in Vanuatu, to shine.' The national football side's home had been constructed with help from FIFA Forward funding.[6] Infantino certainly enjoyed his visit, stripping down to his football kit to play football with Ni-Vanuatu and FIFA legends, and encouraging the country – 165th in the FIFA/Coca-Cola World Rankings – to bring in coaching expertise via FIFA's Talent Development Scheme, an initiative led by FIFA Chief of Global Development Arsène Wenger. Such developmental initiatives are arguably what FIFA really is for; we are, though, more used to seeing the FIFA president at the side of world leaders, as when US President Donald Trump convened the first meeting of his 2026 World Cup taskforce, announcing that the co-hosted event would be the 'biggest, safest and most extraordinary soccer tournament in history',[7] while also generating close to US$50 billion in economic output for the United States.

Family fragility

For all the talk of the 'FIFA family', FIFA, its NFAs and CCs are far from a smooth-running, happy-looking institution. In UEFA, there was a boost to membership after 1991, on the dissolution of the USSR and the creation of a host of newly independent states; the confederation has also granted membership to countries from the

AFC, the prominent example being Israel's move into UEFA from the AFC. Such situations have helped UEFA grow to its current size, though the Russian Federation's NFA was swiftly suspended following Russia's invasion of Ukraine in February 2022. Nevertheless, 'Russia' continues to appear in FIFA's alphabetical listing of 'UEFA Associations'.[8] Following the invasion of Ukraine,

> UEFA and FIFA kicked Russia out of the global game after Poland, Sweden and the Czech Republic refused to play the country, but Russian as well as Belarusian officials have retained a prominent presence in the European confederation ... UEFA said through a spokesman ... that 'the decision of the UEFA Executive Committee to suspend Russia from all our competitions applies to clubs and teams, but it does not concern individuals, players, coaches'.[9]

This 'pass the buck' policy simply further confuses the roles of the NFAs and the CCs.

FIFA habitually quotes from its statutes when it becomes involved in situations such as political interference, and this applies to the statutes of member associations and confederations too. Statute 15 emphasizes that the statutes of member associations must comply with the principles of 'good governance', be 'neutral in matters of politics and religion' and 'be independent and avoid any form of political interference'. The exact wording is repeated in Statute 23, referring to the confederations.[10] Yet behind the scenes, away from the pitch, football administrators are frequently horn-locked in what are essentially political issues. For many of the 211 member associations, for instance, juggling their dual memberships of FIFA and their specific confederation can involve politics.

Nevertheless, Greenland has looked to become FIFA's 212th member association; some of the most committed football enthusiasts in the world have proposed their potential membership of FIFA.[11] Rejected by UEFA, which requires members to be independent states recognized by the United Nations (a principle flouted by the UK which boasts four NFAs), Greenland has a national (men's) team but wants to play better teams, to become recognized among peers rather than existing in a kind of no-man's-land in which its players need day jobs as well as dedicating themselves to the sport's development. They want to be able to show how the game can be advanced, developed for all across the inhabited areas of the world's biggest island. And why not? This seems like an ambition central to FIFA's long-standing mission and objectives. The population is bigger than many of FIFA's NFAs, and it seems to observers and locals that, spurned by UEFA, a place in the CONCACAF among the fellow minnows of the Caribbean and Central America would be a symbol of the authenticity of FIFA's claims. Given FIFA's riches, aid could be provided for the expansion of outdoor and indoor facilities, for accommodation and transport improvements to welcome visiting teams, and help navigate the maritime and air-based modes of transport between the island's cities and communities. Much of this is possible, but the chairman of the Football Association of Greenland had little response when initially seeking to contact CONCACAF board members about an application for membership. Nevertheless, the CONCACAF general secretary invited the Greenland federation to talks in Miami, at the headquarters of CONCACAF; this was rearranged to take place in London in April 2025. It would be a splendid illustration of genuine FIFA/CONCACAF collaboration were Greenland to gain membership; a positive story of football's potential capacity to build and sustain communities, overcome (for short periods of time) ethnocentric and cultural biases, and contribute to collective and individual well-being. By June 2025, though, CONCACAF had rejected the application for membership, and Greenland's football president observed that 'this is not a victory for football democracy'.

Another domain where FIFA's stated values of neutrality, equality and respect have come under particular scrutiny is race. Amid growing pressure to address racist abuse and structural inequality in football, the organization has launched a series of anti-racism initiatives, with mixed results (as discussed in Box 3.1).

So who's in charge?

So who really runs the FIFA game? Europe's dominance of FIFA in its early years, and the stubborn and continuing influence of the European confederation UEFA (formed in Basel in 1954) upon the wider football world, has established a core theme that informs the rest of the book. It is fair to say that the decision-making processes determining who next hosts FIFA's biggest asset, the men's FIFA World Cup, have fallen out of the hands of the NFAs and the committees

Box 3.1: 'Say no to racism – my game is fair play'

On 14 June 2017, in the context of the FIFA Confederations Cup in Russia, FIFA introduced a three-step scheme to combat 'discriminatory incidents'. Observers would be in place to monitor incidents; referees would have the authority to stop a match and call for the cessation of the discriminatory behaviour; the official could then suspend and, step three, abandon the match should the behaviour persist. FIFA sought to uphold its stated 'principles of fair play and to take part in football in a spirit of unity, respect and equality'.[12]

Fatma Samoura, FIFA secretary general, reaffirmed before the Russia 2018 World Cup that there would be 'systems in place to react to and sanction discriminatory acts as well as measures to ensure a discrimination-free environment' at the event.

It remains unclear how effective the FIFA initiative has been, however willing the governing body appeared to be to tackle the issue. Following an 'extensive consultation process' with former and current players said to be 'passionate about making change', FIFA's Bangkok Congress approved a 'Global Stand Against Racism' proposal: 'a five-pillar plan to tackle racist abuse in football'.[13] Pillar one, make racism an offence in the disciplinary code of every member association; two, train referees to use a cross-hand gesture for warnings and decisions; three, recognize racism as a criminal offence in all countries, pushing for sanctions where it's already an offence; four, aspire to a 'future free of racism' by promoting education initiatives with schools and governments; five, establish an anti-racism panel of former players to assess how the plan is proceeding.

This is well meant, but is it more tokenistic than interventionist? Mostly words rather than action? As any experienced football enthusiast knows, racist abuse has not gone away on the football

> terraces of the world, or, less frequently but more visibly, on the field of play. Even when it tries so hard, FIFA seems to fall short.
>
> Football is a game for all, and can foster inter-cultural relations on and off the pitch. As sociologist Ben Carrington emphasizes, sport can help 'communities to live, work and play with and through difference, in an age still marked by the historical scars of Empire and racial exclusion', and 'we need to understand and map the continued importance that sporting spectacles play in giving shape to national identities'.[14]

of the confederations. Gianni Infantino and his 'Bureau of the Council' – a select group of FIFA vice-presidents, including the presidents of the six CCs – seem able, for example, to select and propose individual countries for upcoming events with little consultation or accountability. In this climate, organizational transparency diminishes and even vanishes, open discussion dies, voices are muted. Nevertheless, FIFA finances continue to grow on a global scale and intertwine with the politics of global football governance. The big money helps, and FIFA continues to subsidize football developments and schemes in the NFAs, its member associations, to the tune of 'up to USD 8 million for the four-year cycle (2023–2026)' for each association.[15] This cash flow guarantees the loyalty of the NFA to the governing body. The CCs each receive US$60 million over the cycle; each zonal/regional association claims 'up to' US$5 million per cycle. In Chapter 4 we look at the commercial dimensions that have enabled FIFA to survive and grow in the global marketplace – what Susan Strange has labelled the world of Casino Capitalism.

4
FIFA AND ITS COMMERCIAL PARTNERS

Susan Strange's searing critique of the role of money in the contemporary world, *Casino Capitalism*, was published in 1986, exposing the vulnerabilities and fragility of the international economy as it became embroiled in political corruption, financial fraud, money laundering and bank failures. Underlying this situation, she argued a decade later, is the reality that 'money's fructifying, enabling power for good was matched by its terrible disruptive, destructive power for evil'.[1] This may sound melodramatic but it's a challenging assertion, posing big questions. How and why did FIFA become so entwined with corporate, multinational bodies that would become, as its commercial partners, primary, de facto stakeholders? And has the modernizing FIFA that has replaced voluntarist idealists and amateurs with ambitious entrepreneurs and self-aggrandizing profiteers been good for the people's game?

Modest beginnings

FIFA was slow to respond to the possibility of sponsorship of any kind, even when the International Olympic Committee (IOC) was beginning to attract increased income from 'television money'. In 1961, IOC president Avery Brundage recognized that such monies could provide financial support to the International Sport Federations (ISFs) but was unsure how they should be distributed. It had been assumed by David Cecil (Lord Burghley), IOC Board member and president of the International Amateur Athletics Federation (IAAF) as well as vice-president of the IOC, that distribution of such monies would be decided at the discretion of the IOC Executive Board. The ISFs therefore would receive sums seen as proportionate to their contribution to the Olympic Games. Cecil, British pomposity personified, railed at the thought of giving the ISFs themselves the task of deciding how the income should be divided: 'Heaven forfend that the ISFs should have to decide ... the result would make the Congo [the site of a contemporary civil war] look like a kindergarten.'[2]

Cecil got his way with Brundage, the two of them agreeing 'not to include the International Football (Soccer) Federation (FIFA) in the distribution scheme because the "football people [were] full of money" '.[3] This flimsily evidenced assertion was made in the same year that Stanley Rous began his presidency at FIFA. Sponsor-seeking and commercialism were far from priorities for the new president, for whom coaching schemes and education of referees were the key to international football development. It would be several years before the big money rolled in to football's governing body, and Rous' successor as president, Havelange, gave top priority to growing FIFA's finances. Broadcasting rights and business marketing (corporate sponsorships) income would be combined to establish a more ambitious model, a new framework for sport and football finances; in this, FIFA would be at the front of the queue, its men's World Cup emerging as a magnet for global broadcasters and sponsors.

Finding FIFA funds

FIFA's urgent need for income was prioritized by Havelange, who put pressure on Sepp Blatter – both before and after the Swiss held the position of general secretary at the organization – to find new sources of income and revenues that would enable FIFA to deliver on his manifesto promises. Havelange had made eight pledges in the 1974 manifesto: to increase the number of World Cup final teams from 16 to 24; to create a junior, under-20 World Championship; to construct a new FIFA headquarters, a bold aspiration that he lived to see in FIFA's move into its massive new Zurich HQ in 2006 (Figure 4.1); to provide materials to needy national associations; to help in stadium development and improvement; to set up more courses for professionals; to make available medical and technical help; and to introduce an intercontinental club championship.[4] His commitments to the African and Asian member associations also required financial resources that FIFA lacked.

Havelange turned to Horst Dassler, son of Adolf 'Adi' Dassler (founder of Adidas), the giant German sport company which was to become such a stalwart 'world partner' of FIFA and the IOC. In late 1974 or early 1975 Dassler met with British entrepreneur Patrick Nally – pioneer of modern sports marketing – at his Adidas French base in the Alsace hills. Nally recalls their meeting: 'Dassler foresaw the increasing professionalism of international sports federations and the huge possibilities of television money, and recognized he would have to "go very much more within the system, within the federation system and the IOC".'[5] Nally provides a character reference and an evaluation of the importance of this moment:

Figure 4.1: FIFA headquarters in Zurich

> [Dassler had] a total paranoia that someone was always trying to trip him up. So his whole life was secrecy and looking over his shoulders and spying on the opposition and paying. Everything was intriguing, everything was suspicious. So he would have spies, all of his sports people who were out there to look after the athletes would always spy on the opposition. They'd all be trained to bug telephones. They'd all be trained to go into other people's brief cases ... it WAS the shoe wars. You were out there to do what you could to the enemy. He would keep information, you would get people drunk, you would be trained to investigate and find out what other people were up to.
>
> What Havelange needed was someone to help him make his dreams a reality. The man he went to was Horst Dassler, and the man Horst Dassler went to was me because this was the beginnings of how we would now work with the international federations and how we would get sponsors to come and support world sport.

This might sound straight out of a John le Carré spy story but these dynamics, deals and denials of business ethics were to become the practices that framed the new commercial logic of world sports taking shape in the football industry. Funding was secured for FIFA on the basis of an exclusive deal with Coca-Cola; Nally travelled the world for 18 months negotiating with key figures in the soft-drink corporate giant, including top executive Al Killeen, corporate marketing director and then head of the company's corporate marketing function.[6]

The Coca-Cola Company had a federal structure, and did not typically make central decisions concerning worldwide policy and investments. Nally took Killeen to a match at Brazil's Maracanã Stadium, 'which absolutely blew his mind. He couldn't believe these 110 thousand screaming Brazilians that were there for the warm-up, before the real match'. Thus converted to the marketing and branding potential of a sport that could mobilize commitment and passions on such a scale, and across the globe, Killeen battled inside the company at board level ... and won the decision to:

> agree to do a world-wide sponsorship programme and that all of the various markets would contribute. But it wouldn't be that they were asked, they were told and had to contribute a small percentage of their money to a central pot in Atlanta, which Atlanta would then disperse on this and other programmes.[7]

The Coca-Cola deal was a game-changer, pouring resources into the competitions of the African (CAF) and Asian (AFC) Confederations, and locating new FIFA competitions within those confederations' venues; and most prominently, increasing the number of competing teams by 50 per cent to 24 at the 1978 Argentina World Cup and so attracting new sponsors alongside Coca-Cola.

Nally and Dassler ended their business relationship in 1982 and the following year Dassler set up International Sport and Leisure (ISL), which established innovative financial deals generating new levels of income for sporting bodies, including an ailing IOC on 28 May 1985: 'On that day in Lausanne ...

relief and commensurate celebration ensued as Juan Antonio Samaranch, representing the IOC, and Horst Dassler, representing ISL, signed the TOP-1 (1985–88) agreement.'[8] TOP ('The Olympic Programme') was a sponsorship deal closely based upon the earlier successes of Dassler and Nally in establishing at FIFA the principle of the exclusivity of marketing rights.

For Dassler, ISL was a means of establishing networks in the field of global marketing, alerting the giant global corporates to the rising profile of international sport and to the worldwide visibility that a partnership with FIFA focusing on World Cup events would create. Nally and Dassler had guaranteed exclusivity in all aspects of merchandising and franchising to the interested parties and so offered them a single option only, to buy into the complete marketing package: 'The sums were so vast that lots of companies couldn't touch it but it was a lot easier to work with the few who could.'[9]

In on the action in the money-raising stakes was Sepp Blatter. He had worked at Longines, the watchmaker, before being appointed to the post-Rous 'FIFA family' of no more than a dozen or so people in Havelange's early days. Blatter was initially trained at Dassler's French headquarters in Landersheim. The relationship that he and Havelange developed with Dassler changed the landscape of international sport-based markets across the world, as the continental confederations (CCs) replicated FIFA's marketing models and rights deals in their own regions and territories.

ISL went on to handle both the marketing and television rights for FIFA. In December 1997 a meeting of FIFA's executive committee in Marseilles approved the ISL 'marketing concept', declaring themselves 'entirely satisfied with all the explanations provided with regard to the ISL concept, which has a total value of 420 million Swiss Francs for 2002 and SFR 470 million for 2006, with profit sharing foreseen in excess of these figures'.[10] The comfortable and satisfied FIFA committee little realized that such a windfall would be undermined by the collapse of ISL in 2001. Nevertheless, adopting the US Department of Justice (DoJ) phrasing, the FIFA enterprise continued to enable the implementation of sports marketing bribery schemes that could be exploited well into the 21st century in various forms. The US DoJ vividly shows, in Figure 4.2, the ways that bribery schemes worked.

The schemes operated in quite simple flows. The tournament organizer, FIFA, owns the media and marketing rights, highly sought-after assets. FIFA doesn't go straight to those who want these assets but instead brings in a sports marketing company. The sports marketing company in this case is ISL, whose job is to extract the highest bids from broadcasters for the media rights and from potential commercial affiliates. ISL – Dassler and his team – then report back to FIFA with details of the offer, but not until large sums have been siphoned off from the offers and find their way into the personal bank accounts of individuals – in our case here, via the infamous figure of ISL employee Jean-Marie Weber, known as FIFA's long-term middleman and financial bagman. So the

Figure 4.2: Sports marketing bribery schemes

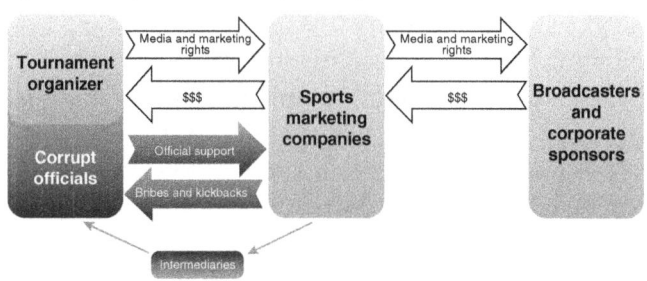

process seems all above board until large chunks of the actual monies are diverted by intermediaries (some of Weber and his team at ISL, and corrupt officials at FIFA, including João Havelange himself) in bribes and kickbacks. Some corrupt FIFA officials, providing 'official support' initially to ISL, returned to base as if the whole transaction was above board. Elements of these procedures were well-established right from ISL's foundation. A Swiss prosecutor's court document, revealed to the public in 2012, confirmed that 'Havelange had indeed taken bribes from the marketing company ISL throughout the 1990s, in return for him selling to ISL FIFA's TV and marketing rights for World Cups'.[11] The document confirmed that 'commission payments' from ISL had been made from its very earliest days, and cited the evidence of chief financial officer of ISL stating that beyond 'the buying of the actual rights to the sporting events' payments must be made 'to individuals who had helped conclude the contract'.

A slush fund had also been established by ISL in neighbouring Liechtenstein, a handy local offshore banking haven, in which by the late 1990s 36 million Swiss Francs had been accumulated as a source for payment of bribes.

The profile of international football was on the rise throughout the 1980s and 1990s, in the form of new competitions in all parts of the world. The outline model of the sports marketing bribery scheme could be adapted on many levels and was to be replicated, for instance, across several of FIFA's CCs in relation to media rights and commercial partnerships; and, as the profile and spectacular scale of the men's World Cup grew and expanded, bidding wars became the order of the day.

On a hot morning in a smart Rome hotel on the day of the Champions League final between Barcelona and Manchester United in May 2009 I met with Jürgen Lenz, former ISL executive and architect of the Union of European Football Associations' (UEFA's) Champions League remake in 1992. We were discussing the ups and downs of Sepp Blatter's presidency, which inevitably touched on the general question of FIFA's status. Lenz's unsolicited comment has haunted me for years: 'FIFA's now so corrupt that it no longer knows that it's being corrupt.'[12]

The collapse of ISL

In the words of Andrew Jennings, FIFA and its close partner ISL established, through Horst Dassler's initial network building,

> an era of corruption ... Dassler paid huge bribes to the ... boss of track and field, Primo Nebiolo, and he paid João Havelange, for 24 years until 1998 ... and in return ... got the exclusive TV and marketing rights to the World Athletics Championships – and the Olympic Games. And best of all, the football World Cup.[13]

It was a global goldmine for sports marketing men and corrupt football administrators across the world.

But the demise of ISL began with the thunderbolt loss of the rights to the Olympic Games in 1995, alongside increasing trends in the sports marketing business to bring expertise in-house. In May 2001 the company was finally 'declared bankrupt at the Zug Court in Switzerland leaving a debt of 300 million dollars'.[14] The consequences for FIFA looked devastating, and its initial response was to seek to find ways of helping ISL survive its crisis; when this failed, FIFA essentially sought to cover up the ISL problem, including the scale of its own losses.[15]

To use one of Blatter's own nautical metaphors, the FIFA boat was rocking and in danger of sinking. A rescue succeeded, via a securitization deal for FIFA. Andreas Herren of the FIFA Communications Department confirmed in 2001 that a tidy US$420 million – the exact projected sum accepted by the FIFA committee back in 1997 – had come in from the Credit Suisse First Boston Bank, the investment bank arm of the Credit Suisse Group.[16] This was quite some success, 'a securitization deal backed by the revenues from the FIFA Marketing Partner Agreements for the

FIFA World Cups(™)'.[17] In Herren's press release he confidently added that 'by using this advanced financial instrument, FIFA has achieved its objective of smoothing the cyclical nature of its revenue stream'.

Blatter could now console all aboard that the family and crew were OK again, and the monies began to stabilize and flow through the financial channels of FIFA, member associations and confederations. Well after Blatter's departure from the FIFA family though, at the end of 2016, Credit Suisse was 'slammed for AML – anti-money laundering – failings linked to FIFA corruption'.[18]

World Cup cycles and commercialization

We saw in Chapter 2 how FIFA's growth spurts indicate the shifting profile of the emergent global and globalizing football phenomenon. FIFA's primary goal in its first phase was to establish an international basis for global football governance, and it also envisaged the formation of an international competition. The international growth of the game across a long second phase from 1921 to 1974 centred around the World Cup: 'Rimet's main achievement was to lead the inauguration of the World Championship World Cup ... first staged in Uruguay in 1930.'[19] From 1974 to 2011, a third phase of FIFA's development prioritized expansion and marketization and at the heart of this was the governing body's increasingly lucrative cash cow, the men's World Cup. Later phases were defined by the scandal of all scandals and the measures then taken to salvage FIFA's credibility and reputation. But through all these phases, the World Cup was the goose that laid the golden egg. David Goldblatt argues that in order to understand clearly the relationship between globalization and the World Cup 'we must divide our narrative into four eras' and that 'since 1982, the World Cups of the most recent era of globalization [are] characterised by new geographies of global power and the unprecedented scale, size and significance of global and financial media networks'.[20]

The geographies, simply conceived, can be seen in a mapping of World Cup venues (see Figure 4.3). By 2034, 23 countries will have hosted or co-hosted the men's World Cup Finals. Mexico, stepping in to take the place of an unprepared Colombia in 1986, will top the leaderboard with three; two-time hosts are Uruguay, Brazil, Italy, France, Germany, Spain, the United States and Argentina; one shot each has gone to Switzerland, Sweden, Chile, England and – the following list from 2002 onwards – Japan, South Korea, South Africa, Russia, Qatar, Canada, Portugal, Morocco, Paraguay and Saudi Arabia.

Western and Central Europe and South America had dominated the early 20th-century history of the World Cup, but FIFA has without doubt in the new century opened up access to the mega-event, with Africa and Asia increasingly making the case for staging the spectacle. Worldwide audiences demand global spectacle and FIFA president Infantino announced to the world in October 2023 that 'the "Greatest Show on

Figure 4.3: Countries that have hosted the men's FIFA World Cup, 1930–2034

Earth" will be organised by Canada, Mexico and the United States in 2026 – in North America'. Expectations would be similar for the co-hosts of 2030 and sole host of 2034, Saudi Arabia. The geographical spread of the event has not, though, offered much challenge to the outcome of the event, as Figure 4.4 indicates.

The growth of the World Cup juggernaut is undeniably spectacular, given that in the inaugural tournament in Uruguay in 1930 just 13 teams competed, a result of European scepticism about the venue, and the costs and difficulties of international overseas travel for anyone outside the Americas. The odd number of 13 competitors was a consequence of the withdrawal of Japan and Siam (Thailand) from a planned starting line-up of 16; the third absentee, the Egyptian team, was delayed by a storm in the Mediterranean and missed a connecting ship leaving Marseilles for South America. The final line-up comprised seven teams from South America, four from Europe and two from North America. The teams made up four groups, one with four teams and the others each with three teams. The hosts defeated Argentina 4–2 in the final, in what in retrospect looks like a tournament pretty much dominated by the Americas. Europe saved face with four teams turning up, but 'even they were not able to send all their best players';[21] rather, top European club teams stayed at home preferring to compete for a Cup of Central European Nations in Geneva. A century on, the World Cup will have expanded far beyond the founders' imaginations, should the proposal – from March 2025 – of one member of the FIFA Council be accepted that there should be 64 teams at the 2030 event.[22]

WHAT IS FIFA FOR?

Figure 4.4: Countries that have won the men's FIFA World Cup, 1930–2022

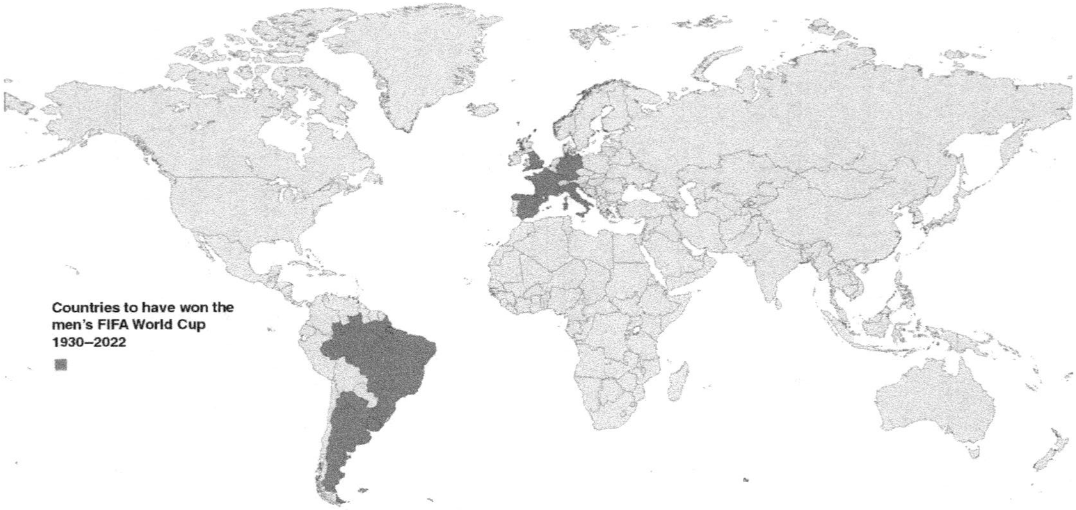

Notes: In South America: Brazil (5 times), Argentina (3), (Uruguay (2). In Europe: West Germany/Germany (4), Italy (4), France (2), Spain and England (1 each).

Spectatorship

No sporting competition lasts for long without the crowd and the World Cup is no exception, as Table 4.1 demonstrates.

In 1998 FIFA expanded a World Cup in France that accommodated 32 finalists and provided 64 matches, but Table 4.2 shows that no host country of the seven subsequent World Cups up to 2022 could report the

Table 4.1: **Spectators at FIFA's first 15 men's World Cup Finals**

Year	Host	Spectators (millions)	Matches	Teams
1930	Uruguay	0.5	18	13
1934	Italy	0.4	17	16
1938	France	0.5	18	15
1950	Brazil	1.3	22	13
1954	Switzerland	0.9	26	16
1958	Sweden	0.9	35	16
1962	Chile	0.9	32	16
1966	England	1.6	32	16
1970	Mexico	1.7	32	16
1974	West Germany	1.8	38	16
1978	Argentina	1.7	38	16
1982	Spain	2.1	52	24
1986	Mexico	2.4	52	24
1990	Italy	2.5	52	24
1994	United States	3.6	52	24

Table 4.2: **Spectators at men's World Cup Finals, 1998–2022**

Year	Country	No of spectators
1998	France	2.8 million
2002	Japan/South Korea	2.7 million
2006	Germany	3.3 million
2010	South Africa	3.1 million
2014	Brazil	3.4 million
2018	Russia	3 million
2022	Qatar	3.4 million

scale of spectatorship generated in the United States back in 1994.[23]

No doubt, the 2026 united bid of the United States, Canada and Mexico as co-hosts is likely to exceed the US's spectator turnout of 1994. With 104 matches played by 48 teams (almost one in four of FIFA's member associations) a new record of spectator attendance can be expected, led by what was in 1994 mocked as the country of the oval ball and little serious soccer.[24]

The future

For the FIFA four-year financial cycle leading up to the men's World Cup 2026, FIFA projected a revenue budget of US$11 billion, and year on year within its anticipated budgeted revenue has confirmed that its expectations have continued to be met: 'FIFA's 2023–2026 budget is aligned with its strategic vision, the aim being to increase football development funds and allow FIFA's international tournaments to flourish.'[25] Of the overall total, television broadcasting rights amounted to US$4.26 billion; marketing rights, US$2.7 billion; licensing rights, US$669 million; hospitality rights and ticket sales, US$3.1 billion; and other revenue and income, US$2.8 billion. This cycle showed 'a substantial increase in revenue of USD 4,560 million' in comparison to the previous cycle.

The tentacles of FIFA and its World Cup now reach across all corners of the globe; FIFA licensed media rights with/for media partners in 133 territories across the world for the World Cup 2026.[26] In Africa the 55 deals struck were all made with FIFA as licensor; as was the case with the 21 deals made in Asia. Across Europe, 45 of the licensor deals were in the name of FIFA, with nine other licensor deals in the mix, mostly the European Broadcasting Union. FIFA was licensor for all five of the deals made in the Oceania grouping. It is in the Americas where FIFA has much less of a presence as licensor, with FIFA holding only 24 out of the 56 named deals.

In the current World Cup cycle the broadcasters and the sponsors seem content enough, their brands prominent in the gaudy promos plastered all over the stadia and around the venue(s). The top sponsors – 'commercial affiliates' in FIFA speak – adorned 'the most effective international marketing platform', this being the 'FIFA World Cup™', as FIFA proudly lined them up for the forthcoming 2026 bonanza. They would all be included in FIFA's six bullet-pointed privileges within its 'standard rights package': use of the Official Marks (intellectual property items); exposure in FIFA's publications and official website as well as in and around the stadium; beneficiaries of a sponsor recognition programme; ambush marketing protection; hospitality opportunities; and lots of promo, ads and 'preferential access to FIFA World Cup™ broadcast advertising'.[27] The top sponsors are: Aramco (energy); Adidas (sports goods); Coca-Cola (official sponsor since 1978); Hyundai/Kia (vehicles); Visa (finance, veteran of 40 events); and Qatar Airways (tied in with FIFA until at least 2030). A newcomer 'partner' was tech all-rounder Lenovo.

These bodies are hugely influential, providing the financial flows that have enabled FIFA to expand their biggest tournaments on unprecedented scales. They are adept in the protection of their brands, framing the stage on which the World Cup spectacle is based: modes of consumption are dictated within the stadium, so that Coke not Pepsi has to be the order of the day, and everyday purchases can only be made by Visa. MasterCard was for 16 years a partner of FIFA, a World Cup sponsor since 1990, and had understood that it would continue as FIFA's selected partner for the upcoming cycle of 2007–2014. At a meeting of its executive committee in late 2005 FIFA had indeed confirmed its commitment to keep working with this favoured long-term business partner.[28] But a year later MasterCard was engaged in a legal action versus FIFA in a US district court in New York. Chief Judge Loretta Preska explained that MasterCard's 'most recent sponsorship contract with FIFA gave MasterCard the first right to acquire the FIFA World Cup sponsorship for the next cycle', but 'FIFA breached its obligation under Swiss contract law' to honour that right.[29] Judge Preska reported further that FIFA's negotiators 'lied to Visa' constantly, assuring Visa that MasterCard had no incumbency rights. A subsequent ruling questioned Preska's judgement but by then MasterCard had had enough of FIFA's shabby business dealings, and in the following year accepted US$90 million in compensation from it. Jérôme Valcke, FIFA's head of marketing, and Chuck Blazer, member of the executive committee and the marketing committee, were singled out in the ruling for their lack of credibility, their lies and evasive responses when questioned in the court. Valcke resigned but soon bounced back as general secretary.

Commercial partnerships have been pivotal in FIFA's expansion, some of them in the FIFA game for the long run, others fitting in to cyclical changes according to regionalized or specifically local markets appropriate to the World Cup venue. The sponsorship and broadcasting models emerged and thrived throughout the 1970s and 1980s and FIFA was able to establish, despite some threatening financial crises, long-lasting 'partnerships' with selected global corporations. In the 1990s the dramatic reshaping of the global media landscape spawned the licensing of new technologies that established a genuinely global reach for pioneering broadcasters, so providing limitless opportunities for sporting bodies to negotiate increasing levels of revenue for the sale of their rights. FIFA could create such partnerships in circumstances almost as it pleased and from its base in Switzerland 'was not accessible to the public ... not accountable to elected public bodies anywhere in the world' and 'not subject to the traditions of democratic governance typically found in the public sphere of Western democracies'.[30]

To conclude this chapter, we can answer the two questions posed at its start. First, FIFA had to find sustainable sources of income, initially to meet the promises of the Havelange manifesto and then to generate expanding numbers of partners and stakeholders in order to underpin its own growth. In doing this it transformed itself from the small administrative not-for-profit operation into a money-making machine and partner of global corporations dominating the new worlds of sports marketing and global communications. And second, given the governing body's vulnerability to forms of exploitation for personal gain by FIFA personnel without impunity, and its capacity to tolerate countless examples of collusion, corruption and criminality in numerous of its national football associations (NFAs) across the world, this has made FIFA's trajectory one that leaves many football followers and enthusiasts disillusioned.

5
'GOOD-LOOKING GOVERNANCE': INVESTIGATING CORRUPTION

Commentators, researchers and scholars have generated significant critical and investigative work on FIFA, creating a composite picture of embedded collusive and corrupt practices in and around the global FIFA family. In 2016 Harvard professor John Ruggie, commissioned by FIFA itself, concluded in his report that '[w]hat is required is a cultural shift that must affect everything FIFA does and how it does it. The result must be "good governance", not merely "good-looking governance". To put it in the simplest terms, FIFA, the global football enterprise, must transform itself into a modern organization'.[1] Has such a transformation been achieved? FIFA's post-2015 reforms, strategies and practices, subjected to particularly powerful evaluations over the last decade by human rights activists and agencies, suggest that 'good-looking governance' – not ethical, transparent principles and practices – remains the order of the day.

The road to corruption

Stanley Rous was not the last FIFA president to do the job for no payment. João Havelange occupied the position without remuneration too. Neither man lived in Zurich, and they continued to spend much of their time at home in London and Rio de Janeiro, respectively. The three European presidents of FIFA to precede Rous throughout the 1950s were from France, Belgium and England and were not salaried. Rous took the position on in 1961 and for a short period carried on living at the Football Association's (FA's) London base, at Lancaster Gate, until former colleagues in the English football world pointed out the absurdity of the situation, and Rous moved to a dwelling a little down the road from his long-term home as the FA's secretary. But still, as far as we can be sure, he took no payment; his FIFA duties across the world were covered by expenses, administered by the conscientious secretary general, Dr Helmut Käser, in the FIFA offices in Zurich. There was little serious money in the FIFA accounts and though some FIFA personnel may have accepted the odd perk or present here and there on international trips or at a FIFA Congress, there is no evidence to suggest that any of the officials or staff at FIFA abused the statutes or cooked the books.

That was to change under Havelange. The small scale of Rous' FIFA operation could not provide the resources and funding needed to achieve Havelange's ambitious goals. International Olympic Committee (IOC) member, successful businessman, and now the man in charge of the whole of world football, he knew how to do deals, make decisions and generate the revenues that were necessary to modernize the FIFA brand; and this included finding new partners, as we saw in Chapters 2 and 4. But there would be a downside to the Havelange strategy, as would be revealed by gumshoe investigative journalist Andrew Jennings.

Jennings could sniff out corruption and tells the tale of Havelange's downfall in his book *The Dirty Game: Uncovering the Scandal at FIFA*.[2] A phone-call from Seoul from a top FIFA executive in May 2002, prior to the forthcoming FIFA Congress and the men's World Cup Finals, alerted him to the fact that five years earlier the caller had 'witnessed Blatter's shock when the bribe for Havelange landed accidentally at FIFA instead of in one of the Brazilian's personal accounts'.[3] Jennings attributes the caller's motivation to having observed for so long how Havelange had operated in a 'blatantly corrupt' partnership with his bagman Jean-Marie Weber, as we saw in Chapter 4. But it took ten more years for Jennings to get his hands on the long-suppressed report by an independent public investigator who was working in line with Swiss public law.

It took the dogged persistence of Jennings and others to sustain the waves of exposure, and he also supported those who sought to speak out from within the FIFA family. One such figure, Bonita Mersiades, must be recognized for her honesty in exposing the hypocritical excesses and the outright lies of FIFA-related personnel and clients who were pursuing the World Cup hosting role. This latter was becoming the holy grail for those who would trust FIFA to give it a few nudges along the way, abiding by 'whatever it takes' – the FIFA way – to win the bidding race for hosting rights. Mersiades worked for two years on Australia's World Cup bid, before being sacked at the beginning of 2010; at the end of the same year, 'the votes for Russia 2018 and Qatar 2022 … caused shock waves across the world'.[4] She bravely spoke out after her dismissal and, even though she had signed a confidentiality agreement, told how she

> went public via The Australian newspaper saying our bid was 'naïve' for trusting in FIFA. … I was also critical of FIFA and its decades of corruption. Like others interested in these issues, I had read Professor Alan Tomlinson and journalists Andrew Jennings, Thomas Kistner and Jens Weinreich. I had also seen people like Blatter, others associated with Oceania football and the Asian Football Federation at fairly close quarters, in addition to my bid experience. The deal-making was a way of life. Too many people had been in charge for too long and change was desperately needed.[5]

Her book reveals in a riveting narrative how the deals were done in the chase for the votes of the FIFA executive committee, and reminds readers that the Russia and Qatar decisions were not the exceptions, more the rule, where 'the FIFA Executive Committee's decision-making was apparently made in their own best interests, rather than the best interests of the game'.[6]

Human rights, FIFA-style

Continuing critical observations and revelations from academics and journalists have more recently been complemented by the contribution of human rights organizations in exposing FIFA's collusive, corrupt and criminal practices. This has been an increasingly valuable addition to our understanding of the flaws and excesses characterizing the governing body's decisions and institutional responsibilities. And an obvious target for such critical voices has been the ways in which the men's World Cup has been allocated to host nations, an old but persisting issue.

The galvanizing moments that attracted the attention of human rights researchers were in 2010 and 2023/2024 respectively, when World Cup hosting rights were granted to the State of Qatar, for the 2022 competition, and to the Kingdom of Saudi Arabia, for the 2034 World Cup – two Gulf states with relatively little football history, endless sources of financial support and dominant political regimes whose commitments to human rights (Qatar's National Human Rights Committee and Saudi's Human Rights Commission) appear doubtful and tokenistic.

FIFA maintains that it has taken the issue of human rights seriously. But its actual support for such rights is woefully sparse. In its 2022 edition of the FIFA statutes, the organization states that 'FIFA is committed to respecting all internationally recognised human rights and shall strive to promote the protection of these rights'.[7] Let's take the context of the Qatar World Cup event in November/December 2022. Qatar is infamously and ruthlessly opposed to any form of homosexuality, and unsurprisingly some players at the tournament, in support of gay rights, planned to wear OneLove armbands. FIFA, though, threatened to discipline any players who wore the armband, making a mockery of its own ineffectual declaration squeezed into a tiny section of its statutes following an extended list of objectives, including the promotion of the game globally 'in the light of its unifying, educational, cultural and humanitarian values'.[8]

The case of exploited labour brought into Qatar to construct World Cup infrastructure has also been a major issue and has been reported on in FairSquare's 50,000-word report, *Substitute: The Case for External Reform of FIFA*,[9] in which Nick McGeehan and his co-researchers offer an overall evaluation of FIFA's hollow human rights policy. Three aims drive their work: to show how FIFA's 2016 reform process was plagued by long-standing structural flaws; to explain how misgovernance at FIFA is linked to its financially opportunistic business model and a *modus operandi* that generates social harms and abuses; and to demonstrate that, as FIFA is incapable of self-regulation, 'its problems can only be resolved by external regulation'.[10] FairSquare concludes that '[i]n reality, FIFA is characterised by mis-governance and a lack of transparency, and the power of its most senior and powerful officials is rooted in a model of patronage that disincentivises ethical conduct'.

In 2023 and 2024 FIFA's most powerful official, Gianni Infantino, and his inner circle tightened their grip on decision-making and power-broking in FIFA, best embodied in the bidding processes for the men's World Cup in 2030 and 2034. Infantino was in his oratorical element shooing the 2030 bid through the evaluation process, in the first case of a World Cup event taking place not just in multiple countries but across continents.[11] Its bid evaluation report –180 pages of glossy text punctuated by images of footballers from across the world – hailed the 'Morocco/Portugal/Spain 2030' bid as having 'the capacity to successfully host the FIFA World Cup 2030'. It simultaneously welcomed an 'Argentina/Paraguay/Uruguay Centenary Celebration bid', confirming 'the capacity of the three countries to host a spectacular Centenary Celebration'.[12]

The bid document for the 2034 World Cup was published in 2024 prior to the December deadline for the hosting decision, the culmination of a strategy whereby the FIFA president guided Saudia Arabia's bid towards a one-man bidding process, putting Saudi forward as the only viable candidate.[13] FIFA general secretary Mattius Grafström writes in the Foreword to this document that the Saudi bid

> can be placed in the context of its own global vision. Saudi Arabia has in recent years been working to transform its socioeconomic landscape by expanding opportunities for growth and fostering a greater global integration.

> The Kingdom is leveraging its pivotal role in the Arab and Islamic worlds, its strong investment capabilities and its strategic geographical position to create a vibrant environment for both local and international investors and establish itself as a global leader.[14]

Grafström nods a reference towards Saudi's own football development but there's little to be excited about here, when the best that can be offered is a reminder of the nation's 'great steps to grow the game at every level', citing the hosting of 'an outstanding FIFA Club World Cup 2023™' – a claim starkly at odds with global perceptions of that event, which many saw as emblematic of FIFA's current entanglement with Saudi Arabia.

The FIFA document is a masterpiece of denial and delusion, claiming an alignment of FIFA's global goals with the Saudi state's Vision 2030, and evasively sidestepping the human rights issue. A new low in the integrity of FIFA may have been reached on 11 December 2024 when Gianni Infantino himself announced online FIFA's approval of and support for the Saudi bid to host the 2034 event. The silent and supine FIFA Council was in attendance online as Infantino confirmed the outcome of this bogus 'competition', thanking the Council for its unanimous support for the event.

Even Sepp Blatter, Infantino's predecessor, permitted argument, debate and lively exchange in face-to-face sessions of his FIFA executive committee. Infantino faced the camera, not the constituency, announcing his own triumph alongside his celebration of the Saudi success – his handling of the process, in individual and relatively informal alliances with confederation presidents, had paved the way for the Saudi bid to be slid through the bidding process with no competition and the vaguest of evidence-based responses in the evaluation process. Journalists and rights campaigners made their voices heard on this process, but their stories, arguments and revelations were doomed from the beginning of the bidding, as Infantino managed the submission timetables and marginalized other potential candidatures from his continental confederations (CCs).

Guardian/Observer journalist Jonathan Wilson was scathing about the whole process, writing several days before the so-called decision day that the outcome would be met within the FIFA body by an 'applause of acclamation' from the president's acolytes, hailing the triumph that was achieved by FIFA and the Saudi bidders with no serious debate and no voting opportunity granted to the FIFA Council or the FIFA Congress.[15] Wilson damned FIFA's World Cup as 'simultaneously the greatest sporting festival on the planet, and a tawdry commercial machine run at enormous human and environmental cost for the benefit of torturers, murderers, exploiters and the unquenchably greedy, scrutiny stymied by the sheer variety of outrage'.

FIFA, rather than acting on behalf of football and its range of constituents, gave voice to a single presidential figure whose intent throughout the bidding process was to align the goals of the organization with the expressed ambitions and priorities of a non-democratic, theocratically oriented state. A cascade of criticisms met the Saudi coronation, expressing concern about FIFA's failure to take seriously the issues of human rights, and the absence of any properly informed and balanced evaluation of the Saudi bid. At the heart of this, too, was the question of the abuse of labour rights.[16]

The Saudi controversy had followed on from the Qatar story of the 2022 World Cup, as well as Russia's human rights record as observed at the end of this chapter. Overall, the consideration of human rights by the bidding countries for the 2030 and 2034 events, and by FIFA itself, has been seriously lacking in precision and focus. A briefing published by Amnesty International in November 2024 concluded, in relation to bids from Saudi and from Morocco/Portugal/Spain, that 'neither bid has adequately demonstrated how they would address key human rights related to the tournaments'.[17] The three countries bidding for 2030 were strongly criticized for treating the issues in an almost casual fashion, the Spanish Football Association, for instance, stating that this would really be the stuff and responsibility of the national government. In the Saudi 2034 case, the Amnesty report emphasized the severity of outstanding human rights risks in the bid documentation: '[T]he likelihood of widespread violations of human rights in Saudi Arabia – for workers, fans, journalists, residents, players and activists alike – are extremely high. ... Without change, critical voices will be repressed, fans will face discrimination and workers will suffer exploitation.

People will die.'[18] High stakes indeed. In its full report earlier in 2024, Amnesty International and the Sports Rights Alliance laid out the necessary actions and, as appropriate, reforms that each of the countries featuring in the 2030 and 2034 bids should undertake. When the 11 December 2024 extraordinary FIFA Congress – online, admitting no journalists or observers – rubber-stamped the two unopposed bids, FIFA demonstrated its contemporary values, anchored in its indifference towards critical analysts and commentators, its lack of transparency, and a tokenistic approach to the serious human rights issues that accompany the making and staging of the global game.

Patterns of behaviour

Up to the end of the 20th century, FIFA's choices as hosts for the men's World Cup were all single national football associations (NFAs) and dominated by Europe and South America. This changed for 2002 when Japan and South Korea staged the first finals tournament based in Asia. It then returned to Europe when Germany hosted the 2006 event. In 2010 South Africa hosted its continent's first – and so far only –World Cup Final, followed by Brazil in 2014. These were in some ways wholly justifiable choices, amplifying FIFA's stated ambition to grow the game globally, create new markets and take the spectacle to venues in the Global South. Russia (2018), Qatar (2022), the United States/Canada/Mexico (2026), Spain/Portugal/Morocco, plus small contributions from three South

American countries (2030) and Saudi Arabia (2034), raise different questions warranting some consideration of whether they represent a significant shift and change in FIFA's approach to World Cup Final choices, and the processes whereby they are made.

FairSquare sees the Russia 2018 World Cup as a test case. As 'the first major FIFA tournament since the 2016 [FIFA] reforms', how would the host country present itself to the outside world? Two years after Russia was awarded the tournament in 2010, the Kremlin imposed restrictions on civil society and journalists; in 2013 the Duma passed a 'gay propaganda law' criminalizing what it labelled the 'promotion of homosexuality among minors'; the Sochi Winter Olympics staged in February 2014 was mired in controversy over state-based support for doping athletes; and migrant workers constructing Olympic sites were widely subjected to abuse. Russia's invasion of Crimea in early 2014, just weeks after the Sochi Olympics, exhibited a violation of international law alongside its human rights abuses at home. Vladimir Putin's Russia was staging the upcoming 2018 World Cup in what was widely seen as 'an aggressively authoritarian state with a recent record of hosting a mega sporting event tainted with reports of serious human rights abuses'.[19] Putin's right-hand man in the bidding process was Vitaly Mutko, a member of FIFA's executive committee from 2009, as a representative of the Union of European Football Associations (UEFA); but also, from 2008, Russia's Minister of Sport, reappointed in 2012 by 'a presidential decree'.[20] Mutko was president of Zenit St Petersburg football club from 1993, and in 1999 secured Gazprom, the world's largest gas extractor, as the club sponsor. As chair of the Russia 2018 Local Organizing Committee, he led the launch of the World Cup logo in 2014, announcing that the inspiration for the design was inspired by 'Russia's rich artistic tradition and its history of bold achievement and innovation'. Blatter was at the launch, adding that the logo represented the 'heart and soul of the country'.[21] But Mutko would not be there to see the World Cup project through; he stood down in 2017 after the IOC banned him from the Olympics for life for his leading role in the state-sponsored doping programme during the Sochi Olympics. Mutko, a Minister of State, had never declared any conflicts of interest to FIFA when he joined the executive committee, but as Russia's deputy prime minister things caught up with him in 2017 when a FIFA review committee barred him from standing for re-election for a place on the FIFA Council, his ministerial role now seen as contravening FIFA's code of ethics concerning political neutrality, a principle in place in 2009, the year of his appointment to the FIFA committee.[22]

The World Cup event itself provided 'zones of permissible hedonism' in a 'temporarily erected ... global digital village', as David Goldblatt writes.[23] Russia's police and security forces allowed public revels and gatherings that were usually forbidden; critics of the regime were banned from protesting in cities that staged matches; urban space accommodated 'scenes of jubilation and hospitality'. For a month, the football spectacle silenced the critics and in a fantastical opening speech Infantino declared: 'As of today, for one month, football will conquer Russia. And from Russia, football will conquer the entire world.'[24]

Qatar, after its 2010 triumph in the bidding race, implemented processes that allowed it to do whatever it wanted, continuing to 'take things to an extreme', such as in the granting of 'citizenship by royal decree' to its footballers and other athletes. Of the 14-strong Qatari squad that defeated Syria 1–0 in a World Cup qualifying game in October 2016, nine were naturalized from eight different countries.[25] Whether it was abuse of workers, neglect of human rights or the recruitment of non-nationals, FIFA sat quietly apart, a silent spectator as much as a regulator and monitor of principles and values. Vani Saraswathi, director of projects at Migrant-Rights.org, predicted that Qatar would 'pull off the World Cup without having to really bring about meaningful change or engage with those most impacted by its laws and policies. Qatar can do the dance with western critics, knowing well that it doesn't have to change anything on the ground'.[26] And FIFA dances to the Qatari tune, doing little to truly intervene.

None of this is to whitewash earlier World Cup events: Benito Mussolini hovered over the 1934 tournament; Argentina 1978 was in the hands of a military junta that murdered tens of thousands of people, 'a history of FIFA-approved image refurbishment that continues today'.[27] But the most recent World Cup bidding processes do appear to represent novel approaches. FairSquare's Nick McGeehan observes 'a new pattern of behaviour' within FIFA:

> It feels very much like Infantino is aping the behaviour of the autocrats whose company he seems to enjoy and shaping FIFA accordingly. Power is increasingly centralised and ad hoc presidential decision-making is effectively enabled by the Bureau of the Council, and increasingly large sums of money are being spent on PR and the promulgation of brand narrative, i.e. 'football unites the world'. On World Cup host selection, the trend is moving clearly in the direction of Presidential selection too, with the 2030 and 2034 votes the first instance of what looks set to become the new model.[28]

6
FIFA AND THE AMERICAS

Though FIFA began life in Europe, the Americas have always been an essential part of its story. Argentina's national football association (NFA), founded in 1893, gained FIFA affiliation in 1912. The first of FIFA's continental confederations (CCs), Confederación Sudamericana de Fútbol (CONMEBOL), was established in 1916 during the First World War, at an inaugural South American Championship hosted in Argentina. The first World Cup took place in, and was won by, Uruguay in 1930, double Olympic football champions in 1924 and 1928. In North America the United States' NFA was founded in 1913 and signed up as a full member of FIFA the following year. The Canadian Soccer Association dates from 1912. It was not, though, until 1961 that the Confederation of North, Central America and Caribbean Association Football (CONCACAF) was formed with a merger of the federation representing Central America and the Caribbean, and the federation representing North

American Football. Football was deeply embedded in the continent's national cultures, particularly in South America, and led the development of an alternative power centre for the emerging global game.

South America

Argentina and Uruguay burst onto the football scene in the later decades of the 19th century: 'It was among the large British communities' in those two nations 'that the game first took root, played in the 1860s on an occasional basis, and by the turn of the century organized into the first leagues to be formed outside the United Kingdom'.[1] Football historian Guy Oliver asserts that '[o]nly the British have been playing the game longer, and few have ever played it better, than the Argentines'.[2]

The Argentine Football Association dates from 30 years on from the birth of the Football Association (FA) in England. The founder was Alexander Watson Hutton, a Scottish teacher and sportsman since considered as 'the Father of Argentine Football'. His team, the 'Alumni', dominated the football scene, accumulating 22 titles between 1898 and 1911 (15 domestic, seven in international competition) before the club was dissolved. On the international front, Argentina and Uruguay contested the first Lipton Cup (named after English tea entrepreneur Sir Thomas Lipton) in 1905.[3] There was a trial run for a South American international championship in 1912, which was then staged in 1916 on a more developed competitive model hosted by Argentina and including Uruguay – the eventual champion – Chile and Brazil. The winners also came up with the breakthrough suggestion that would provide a framework for the future of the worldwide game: 'It was during this meeting that the brainchild of the Uruguayan, Hector R. Gómez, was taken up, and the Confederación Sudamericana de Fútbol, better known as CONMEBOL, was formed, the first sporting confederation on a continent-wide basis.'[4] This would not have been a great surprise to the president of FIFA, Daniel Woolfall, from Blackburn, England, who at FIFA's 1909 Congress in Budapest, offered an insightful synopsis of football's history to date: 'Formerly football was considered the national game of some countries, now this sport had become the game of the world.'[5] A mite premature perhaps, but prescient.

An international competition aimed at bringing together all footballing countries in South America, initially to compete on an annual basis, was a bold and ambitious goal, but by 1927 Paraguay, Peru, Bolivia and Ecuador had joined the confederation. Colombia affiliated in the late 1930s and Venezuela became the final member in the early 1950s. These ten member associations of FIFA still comprise the total membership of the pioneering initiative that established the confederation; and three of the ten have triumphed as FIFA World Cup champions, bringing the men's World Cup home from ten of the World Cup Finals out of 22 held from 1930 to 2022. In FIFA's Coca-Cola World Ranking for the men's international teams (December 2024) five of the CONMEBOL countries feature in the top dozen, Argentina sitting atop the list after its memorable victory over France at Qatar 2022.[6]

The South America–Europe rivalry would be established not just on the pitch, but in the back-rooms and corridors of power of the confederations and FIFA headquarters. This rivalry was also reaffirmed and amplified when the Europe-dominated FIFA supported the formation of the Union of European Football Associations (UEFA) in 1954. To the South Americans this looked like a threat to their status, the development of an additional power centre to push European interests and avoid South America becoming too powerful. The rivalry continues unabated. In 2025, as many commentators and football fans were critiquing FIFA's newly revised men's Club World Cup (CWC), in South America 'the birth of this type of competition is seen as a dream come true'.[7] The Brazil football calendar, for instance, was specially altered, shutting down the league for a month, to allow clubs time to prepare for the event.

North America, Central America and the Caribbean

CONCACAF was formed in Mexico City in 1961 and based in Guatemala City for 31 years, after which it relocated to New York. The confederation was created through the merger of the North American Football Confederation and the Central American and Caribbean Football Confederation. Stanley Rous, fresh to his FIFA presidency, saw the new body as 'effective' rather than strong, and under the primary influence of

Mexico. The presence of the United States in a revised and expanded confederation was also seen by FIFA as a way of balancing the power and influence of Mexico.[8]

The new CONCACAF could welcome North America/ the United States into the ambitiously expanding confederation, offer football officials opportunities for huge power and influence not just in CONCACAF itself but as members and chairs of FIFA committees, as was the case with Guillermo Cañedo who became João Havelange's senior vice-president at FIFA, chairing its media committee and, in his final act, also heading the organizing committee for the US 1994 World Cup. Rous had wanted to strengthen the rookie confederation, but had not anticipated the level of power-broking that would emerge as the likes of Cañedo combined his football interests with his entrepreneurial media interests as an executive at Mexican media giant Televisa. When Colombia withdrew from its hosting role for the 1986 World Cup, citing economic reasons, the bidding process was rerun: 'Mexico defeated the US. Every vote on the FIFA Executive Committee went to Mexico' and Cañedo's 'courtship of FIFA executives' included the promise of more lucrative rights and marketing deals than previously on the table.[9] CONCACAF was shaping the mould that would embed forms of collusion and criminality that were exposed in the FIFA 2015 scandals.

Andrei Markovits observes that in the United States there was little early enthusiasm for the game, though it thrived in particular ethnic and working-class communities (most notably, among Latinos and immigrants from Europe), and also featured in some colleges in the later 1800s, before giving way to 'the evolution of American gridiron football'.[10] Markovits further observed that when the 1986 World Cup was won by Argentina in a 3–2 victory over Germany, it 'failed to capture the imagination of the American public', adding that American interest in 'the world's most important media event [was] strikingly minute in comparison to that exhibited in virtually every country in the world'.[11] The North American Soccer League (NASL) – at its peak inspired by the availability of the likes of Brazil's Pelé at New York Cosmos, Portugal's Eusebio, Cruyff from the Netherlands and Germany's Beckenbauer – ran from 1968 to 1984, but player recruitment deteriorated and finances imploded in the later years. Therefore a decade or so before the United States staged the 1994 World Cup, it had no men's professional soccer league. It was an opportunity for FIFA president João Havelange, seeing great commercial potential, to take the World Cup for the first time to a host that was not European or South American.

The United States' Big Three, or Four, have dominated the sporting landscape for generations: American Football, baseball, basketball, and, always knocking on the door, ice-hockey. Association football – or soccer – has been the poor cousin in the enriched extended family of primarily male professional team sports. Yet when Havelange's FIFA took the World Cup to the United States, it attracted the biggest attendance ever, a record still unbroken at the time of the tournament's return to North America.

For the then general secretary Sepp Blatter, things couldn't have turned out better: 'The 1994 World Cup produced a turnover of $4 billion with 32 billion television viewers. I mean no disrespect to other sports by saying that even the Olympic Games cannot compare. The World Cup was a fabulous success.' The primary criterion for Blatter, cited in *World Soccer* in December 1994, was essentially economic; and he, along with Havelange, was not alone in emphasizing this. US entrepreneurialism fuelled the bid to stage the event, entrepreneurs from the 1984 Los Angeles Olympics bringing expertise to the project. Most prominent among such figures was Alan Rothenberg, pictured in Figure 6.1, who had the role of commissioner of football for the LA Games, and believed that the sport could attract massive new audiences in well-established venues such as the Rose Bowl, where 100,000+ sell-outs were achieved in the summer of 1984. FIFA saw at the LA event the potential for the staging of the World Cup, and in 1988 confirmed the choice of the United States as host. FIFA also secured Rothenberg as director of the 1994 World Cup, backing him too to take over the chairmanship of the United States Soccer Federation (USSF). Once in position, he was named chairman of the World Cup 1994 Organizing Committee and targeted large venues to match his ambition to elevate football in the United States as an established global spectacle. Rothenberg was clear about his vision, telling one British journalist that 'the World Cup was dead in the water when I came in … there was even talk about taking it away from America'.[12] Labelled by veteran football writer the late Brian Glanville as 'the Czar of American Soccer', 'Alan "£7 million and more" Rothenberg' and FIFA chief Havelange had 'much in common ... neither has any real feeling for the game'.[13] After the World Cup, Rothenberg also took on the position of heading up a new professional league, Major League Soccer (MLS), getting funding from World Cup USA (chair, Rothenberg) and from the USSF (chair, Rothenberg). MLS beat two other bids to set up the national league and then accepted another substantial handout – US$3.5 million – from Rothenberg's own World Cup USA. Questionable as some of these financial transactions might seem, they undoubtedly put in place a body that could benefit from the financial flows of the World Cup.

The 1994 World Cup clearly marked a turning point for the profile of the game in the United States. Three questions, at least, have been posed as to what might remain after the circus leaves town. First, how was an event on such a scale made possible, particularly as at the time soccer looked unquestionably minor league? Second, what has been the impact of the successful staging of the tournament on US sport culture? And, third, has there been any significant impact upon the game itself?

First, the spectacle was made possible by interlocking alliances of world sport bodies which were conducive to staging the event in the United States, and of course this involved sponsors, financial bodies and an increasingly global-conscious media industry, all

Figure 6.1: Alan Rothenberg, smooth entrepreneur par excellence, relaxing in Hotel Le Bristol Paris at the France 1998 World Cup

of which could bring expertise from management of high-profile events such as the Olympics. Second, as we look back over three decades, the impacts on US sport culture have become increasingly visible and FIFA has, as we will highlight at the end of this chapter, invested extensive resources in the United States; this includes events, from the revised CWC of the summer of 2025, the successful US-led combined bid for the men's 2026 World Cup, to a likely US-led Women's World Cup, along with CONCACAF members, in 2031. And third, the 1994 World Cup stimulated FIFA to address concerns about on-field issues such as the protection of players' creative skills and a focus on attacking play. And, overall, 1994 showed, arguably, that a host country outside of the competing elite could successfully host a global event. South Africa, Japan/South Korea, Qatar, in their different ways, have convinced FIFA that this is far from impossible.

MLS is one legacy from the 1994 World Cup that has proved a success – for the moment at least. There were mixed views on whether the World Cup would generate resources and adequate interest to make a go of an ambitious project framed to fill the gap that was created by the dissolution of the NASL. Jon Arnold, though, reflecting in early 2025 on the last 30 years of the MLS, has argued that the ghost of the NASL collapse haunted the business plan of the embryonic MLS, whose primary 'goal, then, was to avoid the errors of the past and become sustainable, something it appears to have done'.[14] And it did this initially as the US soccer scene experienced a boom in venue development and stadium building, creating more appropriate venues to which fans and players could relate, rather than 'the cavernous stadiums shared with American football teams'. Critically, more of the matchday revenues could be re-invested into the clubs themselves.

Evidence of the relative success of the MLS, in its format of 29 teams in the single league including three (Montreal, Vancouver and Toronto) from Canada, lies in the spectator figures: 'very good crowds of passionate fans' congregate 'in nearly every MLS stadium', and the league announced at the end of 2024 that '12.1 million spectators had attended MLS matches in 2024 – the second-best figure in the world behind only England's Premier League (14.6 million)'.[15] A thirtieth team further expanded the league in the 2025 season with the addition of San Diego FC.

This level of success has also been based in canny marketing strategies, stimulated by financial problems and the threat of bankruptcy in 2001. Soccer United Marketing was created as the league's marketing arm and generated revenues and financial ventures boosting the profile of the game, allowing scoops on a global scale such as, in 2007, LA Galaxy's signing of David Beckham from Real Madrid on a five-year contract. Beckham's arrival, it is widely agreed, 'started a new era of Major League Soccer'.[16] And then there was Lionel Messi, brought into the MLS picture in July 2023 at Beckham's Miami the year following his success as World Cup winner in Qatar. There may, though, be a serious competitor to MLS in the United Soccer League, which, in February 2025, announced the launch, planned for 2027, of its own top division, creating a league pyramid, potentially with promotion and relegation. This has the backing of the US national soccer federation, the USSF, and contrasts dramatically with the MLS model of celebrity-based franchises.[17]

Meanwhile, much had been happening in the furthest south-east corner of the United States, where Beckham's Inter Miami is based. CONCACAF has been there too since November 2018; Gianni Infantino was at its inauguration and 'gave a ringing endorsement of CONCACAF ... It's a great honour to be in this global city and to be a part of ... this new and modern headquarters ... which says what CONCACAF is all about ... it represents a new chapter of football in this wonderful region'.[18] Six years later, local journalist Michelle Kaufman reported that FIFA itself had moved into town as well, establishing its Legal and Compliance Office in Miami, so enabling FIFA to reach '10 MAs [member associations] in South America and 35 MAs from North America, Central America and the Caribbean'. Kaufman neatly sums up the FIFA initiative, seeing in the overall picture that proximity to the Americas might well be particularly critical in this moment of moments, with the 'United States hosting the recent Copa America, the 32-team Club World Cup in 2025 and co-hosting the expanded 48-team 2026 World Cup with Mexico and Canada', all adding up to a new scenario in which

> FIFA, the four best-known letters in global soccer, are now visible from atop a prominent Coral Gables office building and a World Cup 2026 display graces the lobby, the latest evidence that the Miami area in recent years has become the epicenter of the sport in the United States and the rest of the Americas.[19]

CONCACAF's primary base is just down the road, at the heart of this emerging power centre of global football. A family residence of President Infantino appears to be there too, switched from Qatar to Miami. At the end of 2024 Swiss media reported that the Miami-based schooling costs of one of Infantino's daughters, $5,000 per month, was being paid for by

FIFA.[20] The revised and expanded CWC, squeezed into the global football calendar from mid-June to mid-July 2025, also raised the profile of Miami and FIFA's base in the city made it a close neighbour to CONMEBOL as well as to a CONCACAF that stretched its membership across the Caribbean. FIFA had also favoured the United States early in Gianni Infantino's presidency, bonding with the US president in the process.

The 'United Bid'

In June 2018 at the 66th FIFA Congress in Moscow, rookie FIFA president Infantino announced the outcome of the bidding process for the 2026 men's World Cup. The hosting rights went to a North American combined bid known colloquially as the 'United Bid', comprising the United States, Canada and Mexico. Its single rival was Morocco, garnering a mere 65 member association (NFA) votes against the United Bid's 134. On the day before the Moscow vote, the *New York Times* revealed that for two or three months leading up to the decision date another president, Donald Trump, had been writing letters to Infantino expressing support for the United Bid 'in the spirit of continental partnership': in these letters 'Trump assured FIFA officials of visa-free travel, that his hard-line stances on visas and his Muslim travel ban would not apply, and agreed to grant FIFA full tax-exemptions on all commercial activity during the tournament'.[21] The key figure co-ordinating Trump's lobbying and letter-writing was his son-in-law and White House adviser Jared Kushner. His active lobbying included discreet trips to Saudi Arabia and Bahrain, and working with the United Bid leaders to set up meetings with 150 of FIFA's 211 member association presidents. Hardly a coincidence, Kushner's mission in Saudi Arabia 'coincided with a signed agreement by the Trump administration to provide military arms to the Kingdom'.[22]

The joint bid was branded by FIFA as one of 'firsts': '[T]he first time the tournament has a 48-team format (up from 32 teams); the first to use already existing world-class stadiums, facilities and infrastructure; and the first time three countries have shared the world's most prestigious and widely viewed football tournament.'[23] The United Bid also promised FIFA an US$11 billion turnover: 2026 would feed the public with 80 matches. Early rounds would stage games in Canada and Mexico (ten each), and the United States would have the lion's share of 60 games, including all games from the quarter-finals to the final. Presidents Infantino and Trump, two years into FIFA's 2016 reforms, celebrated a shared victory which was in violation of FIFA's principles and statutes relating to lobbying expenditure and direct, undue political influence on the outcome of the bidding process.

7
FIFA IN AFRICA AND ASIA: CHALLENGES AND CONSTRAINTS

After his departure as manager of the English men's national team in 1962, Walter Winterbottom reflected on the future of the game: 'Watch Africa. That continent will produce the world champions before the end of this century.'[1] He had seen the potential of the top African teams but his prediction remains unfulfilled. FIFA president Sir Stanley Rous declared in 1963 that many countries established in the post-colonial period in Africa and Asia 'clamoured for membership of FIFA and a place in the international football sun'.[2] How then have FIFA and the Asian (AFC) and African (CAF) Confederations fared in the power games that have ensued?

Africa

Issa Hayatou, a short-term interim FIFA president following Sepp Blatter's resignation, was CAF president from 1988 to 2017, and observed in 1997 that 'the main problem facing African football' was 'the instability of the federations caused by the interference of governments. This is a problem for the majority of federations in Africa. We are trying with FIFA to control this'.[3] Rivalries within CAF among its 54 member associations have also long created problems for a CAF united in principle but sub-divided into five regional federations: North, West, Central, East and Southern Africa.

Hayatou's observation rings true in the case of Kenya. In 2004 the Kenyan sports minister's attempt via a Kenyan High Court ruling to establish a transitional caretaker committee to replace corrupt officials of the Kenya Football Federation was rejected outright by FIFA, on the grounds that this constituted 'government interference in football'.[4] But FIFA's intervention achieved little. Indeed, David Goldblatt sees the Kenya story as 'a casebook study' of FIFA's inadequacies:

> [The] culture and practice of corruption were so widespread that it is hard to describe the management style as anything other than looting. Not a penny was banked from dozens of national team games and their ticket receipts. FIFA monies were totally unaccounted for. Meetings, minutes, audits simply did not happen.[5]

The challenge of improving governance of the whole continent was recognized when in 2019 FIFA stepped in to oversee CAF, relocating its own General Secretary, Senegal-born Fatma Soumara, to CAF headquarters in Cairo, in a new role as High Commissioner or 'general delegate for Africa'. The declared primary goal was the improvement of the confederation's governance role. There's little evidence that this intervention achieved much and Soumara terminated her seven-year spell at FIFA at the end of 2023. The BBC World Service journalist Piers Edwards has observed the African football scene for decades, and concludes that, despite genuine grassroots enthusiasm, and the public passion of supporters of the established clubs, the administration and governance of African football is tainted, widely open to forms of corruption. His report (August 2023) on the Mali football executive Mamatou Touré – FIFA Council member, CAF executive committee member and Mali Football Association (FA) boss 'set to win' Mali's FA election from his base in a prison cell makes gruesome reading.[6] Touré was re-elected, but 17 months on he still awaited trial for charges against him for embezzlement during his time as financial and administrative director in Mali's National Assembly. CAF boss Patrice Motsepe failed to convince Mali authorities that Touré should be released from jail. In January 2025 Touré withdrew from the FIFA Council.[7]

Experienced journalist Brian Oliver, of *The Observer*, wrote in 2010 of the embedded culture of corruption – vote-swapping, match-fixing, bribes – across the continent, quoting a top Zimbabwean coach: 'Nobody dares touch these looters [corrupt football executives] because of the FIFA policy of non-interference. ... The football community will never get to the bottom of the rot.'[8] Bob Munro, vice-chairman of the Kenyan Professional League, noted that it is the 'innocent clubs, coaches, players and referees who suffer most', asking: 'What judicial or other regulatory process in the world punishes the innocent victims?'[9]

At the same time as Soumara was exiting the picture, Gianni Infantino supported a proposal for a new African Football League tournament, a form of super league, launched in October 2023 'as the supposed panacea to all ills besetting football on the continent' as Mark Gleeson, doyen of African football history, reports. A super-wealthy FIFA might have created a participatory model on an inclusive basis, drawing in clubs from all the five sub-regions, generating cross-border encounters at accessible prices that would attract new audiences and followers. But such distributive frameworks were not on FIFA's priority list. Elite clubs were proffered huge levels of prize money as a magnet for their participation and an apathetic public looked away. Apart from the Saudi Tourist Board, sponsors and broadcasters didn't bite. And the media pretty much ignored the final between mining magnate billionaire owner and CAF president Patrice Motsepe's club Mamelodi Sundowns and Wydad Casablanca. Interest was so low that the fans were granted free entry: 'Infantino then hailed the full house for the decider ... as proof of the validity of the project. It was egomaniacal folly from the FIFA president in a subservient forum where his patronage is all-powerful.'[10]

Following the initiative, nothing more was heard of the African Football League, a super league disappearing 'almost as quickly as it rose', an expensive experiment that 'came from FIFA's coffers and the vanity of Infantino's thinking. Motsepe willingly went along. After all, his club won the event and pocketed $4 million'.[11] For Motsepe it had clearly been worth getting the event off the ground.

Africa's four top clubs reportedly reaped US$50 million each for turning up in the United States in the summer of 2025 for Infantino's larger-still new project, the Club World Cup (CWC). Excluding those in South Africa, the majority of clubs on the continent would continue to be 'controlled or funded by state organizations: armies and police forces, city and regional governments, ministries of state and national oil and mining companies. None of this is good for football governance'.[12]

Asia

The AFC was founded in 1954 in Manila, Philippines, and in 2000 settled for the long term in a purpose-built facility in Kuala Lumpur, Malaysia. It has five sub-regional bodies: Southeast, Central, East, South and Western.

Asia's dominant international men's teams are Japan and South Korea, and the Gulf states Saudi Arabia, the United Arab Emirates and Qatar. Japan and South Korea, co-hosts for the 2002 men's World Cup, performed soundly in the tournament, Japan reaching the last 16, South Korea making it to the semi-final. Both teams have good records of progressing through the group stage. Japan's women's team has played in all tournaments since the 1991 opener, winning the 2011 trophy and finishing as runner-up in 2015. South Korea's women have advanced to the knockout stage just once, in 2015. Unsurprisingly, the Gulf states do not have much of a record for their women: a Saudi national team played its first match in 2022, and will no doubt be aiming to represent the nation – whatever the acknowledged status of women in that country – in future tournaments. Qatar's women's football team has been invisible since 2014, after playing a mere 15 official matches since 2009, the year before the successful bid for the Qatar World Cup. After the 2022 event the squad was said to 'exist in some form ... believed to gather for training and matches played in private'.[13] The United Arab Emirates women's team won back-to-back titles in the West Asian Football Federation's championship, in 2010 and 2011. The Saudi men's team, backed by the oil-rich state, has been prominent since the late 1970s, with an infrastructure including at the time 200 or more officials dedicated to the development of the national football confederation:

> The effective boss of Saudi soccer ... was Abdul Fatah
> Nazer, brother of the Saudi oil minister. Fatah was
> a football fanatic with a doctorate from Manchester

University and a collection of British television's *Match of the Day* videos. ... Football was run at the highest level of the nation's elite.[14]

The English Football Association (FA), mounting a losing bid to stage the 2006 World Cup, learnt a lot about such elites. The British government's network of ambassadors and high commissioners reported back to base that the two FIFA executive committee votes, from Saudi Arabia and Qatar, would not be taken by 'the FIFA members but by their governments and ruling royal families'.[15] The Saudi template has become the way forward for similarly ambitious Gulf neighbours.

Malaysian Peter Velappan, General Secretary of the AFC from 1978 to 2007, was a visionary. In his AFC and FIFA-related role he pointed to the need for a more professional approach to football management at national football association level, alongside an 'improved and efficient communication system' that could reach all corners of the AFC. He brought FIFA and the AFC together to work closely in assisting the national associations, introducing various programmes, seminars, study tours and inspection visits, and looking to 'ensure that the National Associations are professionally managed, the leagues well-structured and the various programmes implemented'.[16] His vision comprised: research, plan, produce, market. The problem with visions is that they are rarely pursued on the basis of unanimous consensus, and there is little that the football administration can do when, as Velappan observed, across the South-East

Asia countries 'large-scale gambling has become a professionally organised syndicate operating at national and international levels'.[17]

Velappan stressed too the importance of combating corruption. Illegal betting, including match-fixing and player involvement in betting on the outcome of games, should be tackled by FIFA, he advocated. He also condemned the bribery and corruption becoming prevalent in 'The Big Four' Gulf states – Kuwait, Saudi Arabia, Qatar and the United Arab Emirates – for instance, 'importing' African players, giving them citizenship, and going on to bribe referees, team officials and players. The sheer scale and diversity of the AFC ensures that Velappan's vision will not be shared by all. Bill Murray reminded us that 'the Asia/Oceania group accounts for almost half of FIFA's registered players', and these are spread across the continent with little to connect the different countries and leagues.[18] In Box 7.1 a widely experienced football administrator – whose anonymity must be respected – reflects on this conundrum.

The issues of size, scale, access and communication add up to an underlying problem to which there seems no easy solution. Meantime, Qatar, based to a great extent on players given fast-track Qatari citizenship, has won the Asian Cup for two championships in a row, in 2019 in the United Arab Emirates, and again in 2023 the year following its controversial staging of the men's World Cup. The growing power of the Gulf states shows no sign of slowing down. 'Brand Saudi is deeply flawed', asserts Samindra Kunti, spending, as Human

> **Box 7.1: Why the giant confederations need to regionalize – a football administrator's view**
>
> 'The first point about FIFA, about Asia, and the same applies to Africa, is that they are way too big to be football confederations. Why would you have an entity that spans 12 time zones, 10,000 kilometres or whatever it is? Well, the reason is because it's a political body, not a sporting body. But then they decided to organize competitions; 'Well, in Europe and South America it works, so let's do the same thing; we'll organize competitions across the whole continent'. So with the exception of the Afcom, which is quite popular, pretty much all the other competitions organized by the confederations in Asia and Africa generate little interest. In the big picture, obviously, you'll get some matches between a team from Egypt and a team from Tunisia that sell out ... so, from their creation in the 1950s they've been trying to ram this square peg into a round hole, and it didn't work. It hasn't worked, and it will never work until they regionalize – which is quite reasonable because you already have regional associations in existence.'[19]

Rights Watch observes, 'billions of dollars hosting major entertainment, cultural and sporting events as a deliberate strategy to deflect from the country's image as a pervasive human rights violator'.[20]

As FIFA's men's CWC kicked off in mid-June 2025, the deepening involvement of Saudi Arabia in FIFA matters – including funding, sponsorship and broadcasting options – was confirmed. A project planned by Gianni Infantino since his ascent to the

FIFA presidency, the CWC's 'gold-plated trophy [was] designed by FIFA, crafted by Tiffany & Co', and bore Infantino's signature/name three times.[21] But less than a year before the tournament was to take place, monies were far from forthcoming; the Saudi Arabian state then stepped in and courtesy of its Public Investment Fund (PIF) broadcasting deals were struck, and funding for the competing clubs provided. As the event got off to a lukewarm start, investigative reporter Chris Dalby published a catalogue of ways – 18 in all – in which Saudi Arabia in effect 'bought the Club World Cup ... They own a club, they sponsor the tournament, they provide the prize money, they own the media rights, they fly players in, and it's just the beginning ... Saudi Arabia's presence is not just significant, it's systemic'.[22] When Saudi's Al-Hilal defeated the (England) Premier League's Manchester City on the way to the quarter-finals of the competition, the PIF monies looked well spent. Al-Hilal then lost to the ageing Brazilian team Fluminense, but the Saudi brand and message kept leaping out at the global audience courtesy of the free DAZN screening: 'Saudi, Welcome to Arabia: This Land is Calling', and the revolving stadium ad: 'PIF ... Invested in Better'.

Look away

Infantino watched Paris Saint-Germain humiliate Real Madrid in the semi-final, seated next to Nasser bin Ghanim Al-Khelaifi, chair of Paris Saint-Germain, Qatar Sports Investments, the Union of European Football Associations (UEFA)-affiliated European

Club Association and member of the CWC organizing committee. After Chelsea tamed Paris Saint-Germain in the final, Infantino and President Trump baptised the revised, expanded event, seen by the FIFA president as 'already the most successful club competition in the world'.

Rather than over the years exploring the dynamics underlining the growing influence of power-grabbing Gulf states, or the sources of recurrent corruption in African cases, contemporary FIFA shows little interest in its own declared principles of objectivity, transparency, integrity and human rights.[23] On the contrary, forms of collaboration with selected stakeholders look to be shifting towards collusion and a lack of transparency and integrity. To many, this is certainly not what FIFA was for. The development of the women's game, the theme of the following chapter, may provide a more positive take on the values of the world governing body.

8
FIFA AND THE WOMEN'S GAME

The profile of the Women's World Cup has risen dramatically over the period of nine Finals from 1991 to the event hosted by New Zealand and Australia in 2023, which was widely acknowledged as an outstanding success. FIFA itself, in its report *Beyond Greatness*, identified a 'record-breaking tournament of firsts' for the FIFA Women's World Cup. These included the staging of the event in two countries, which also represented two confederations; the hosting of a senior FIFA tournament in Oceania; 32 teams playing 64 matches; record attendance of almost two million; and a revenue of US$570 million, which meant that the event broke even. FIFA's Technical Study Group lead pointed to impressive developments on the pitch: 'Progress is the biggest story of this tournament so far. Emerging nations are showing they can compete at this level and the gaps with the top teams are closing.'[1] In this chapter we consider both how much FIFA has done for the women's game to achieve such progress, and how much more there is to do.

Pioneers

If there is a single influence that can be highlighted as the most significant factor holding back the development of football for women, it is quite simply: men. In London in 1894, suffragette footballer Nettie Honeyball founded the British Ladies football team, taking on the positions of both club secretary and captain. Around 30 members of the team trained twice a week, and the first public match in March 1895, between the North and South British Ladies teams, attracted over 10,000 spectators. A second game took place in Preston Park, Brighton, the following month, again with over 10,000 spectators. Honeyball (not, it turned out, her real name) saw women's football as an effective form of cultural politics: 'I founded the association ... with the fixed resolve of proving to the world that women are not the ornamental and useless creatures men have pictured.'[2] The British Ladies initiative would last just three years or so, and faced widespread ridicule from a male-dominated press. But women continued to play the game and this generated the Football Association (FA)'s first-ever attempt, in 1902, to ban women's football, forbidding their own members from playing against women's teams. There was, of course, no FIFA in existence at that time, and when the exclusively male FIFA was established two years later, the question of women's participation in the sport was not remotely of interest to the global governing body. It would take a world war to bring out the further potential of the women's game in the UK.

In the Lancashire cotton town of Preston, women did play football, in its modern codified format, under the name Dick, Kerr Ladies Football Club. It was formed during the First World War, when local women took on factory jobs as men went to war; the women took to the game, other teams and sides were formed and matches attracted large paying crowds, generating contributions to specific charities, during and beyond the war.

The story of Dick, Kerr Ladies is a compelling narrative of the against-the-odds triumph of determined women over the controlling men of the post-First World War period. England's FA opposed developments in the women's game, issuing an edict banning the use of the pitches/grounds of FA-affiliated clubs.[3] Despite the popularity and excellence of the football, the Preston side faced intensifying hostility from a 'male soccer establishment' which resented 'the sheer size of the crowds women's football, and in particular Dick, Kerr's matches could attract'. Author Gail Newsham's summative critique says it all: 'Despite the fact that worthy charities were benefiting from the ladies' matches, the uncomfortable truth was that they were drawing bigger crowds than the men, and the boys simply didn't like it. The green-eyed monster was getting closer to the surface.'

The big boys did not want to share or offer support to these pioneering women footballers. Medical 'experts' were approached, who stated that football was 'a dangerous pursuit for ladies to follow'. Class distinction too was at work in this conflict; why, for instance, could women be allowed to play hockey, 'wielding a big stick', but not football? Class and gender combined in the power play that was to undermine the women's game. The FA's Council at its all-male meeting early in December 1921 passed a resolution that has stained its reputation for a century:

> Complaints having been made as to football being played by women, the council feel impelled to express their strong opinion that the game of football is quite unsuitable for females and ought not to be encouraged.
>
> Complaints have also been made as to the conditions under which some of these matches have been arranged and played, and the appropriation of receipts to other than charitable objects.
>
> The council are further of the opinion that an excessive proportion of the receipts are absorbed in expenses and an inadequate percentage devoted to charitable objects.
>
> For these reasons the council request clubs belonging to the association to refuse the use of their grounds for such matches.

No appeal to the FA was permitted but the Dick, Kerr club played on, supported by the sympathetic and supportive – albeit male – company/employer in its search for alternative playing areas/pitches. Not all men approved of the FA ban, though, and the mayor of Burnley, Edwin Whitehead, wrote to the works manager at the engineering company, saying 'I love your team of Preston lasses, and whenever I find them within a measurable distance of Burnley you may rest assured I shall be at the match if at all possible.' In a groundbreaking tour of Canada and the United States at the end of 1922 the Dick, Kerr Ladies, playing teams of men, helped raise the profile of the women's game in the United States in particular, and Burnley's former mayor Whitehead reiterated his support for the women, stating that he was sorry that the FA had banned women's football, and hoped that the governing body would soon acknowledge its mistake and withdraw the ban. Unfortunately, the obstinate and misogynistic males at the FA Council would do no such thing.

The Dick, Kerr club soldiered on sustaining the case for women's football, but folded in 1965 due to the lack of players. The FA rescinded its ruling only in 1971, leaving the newly formed Women's Football Association, established two years earlier, to administer the game until 1993 when at last the FA acknowledged its responsibility for the development and governance of women's football. The ban, in England, had been in place for a full half-century.

Rising profiles

The women's game has evolved almost beyond recognition over the last 25 years, particularly in the big events of the international calendar. The United States has dominated the gold medal podium with five Olympic triumphs out of eight since the first women's event in 1996, and has four World Cup trophies out of the nine tournaments that have taken place since 1991.

No other national team has come close to contesting this scale of domination of the top tier of the sport.

The women's game in the United States shows how at the national level the game could be successfully supported and developed. Women's soccer in the United States was helped along by the Title IX federal legislation, approved in 1972 (though with no mention of sport in the declaration), which opened doors and possibilities for women and girls across the country, providing opportunities to play soccer at higher and higher levels in colleges and universities. With the United States Soccer Federation (USSF) firmly supportive of the development of the women's game, the quality of elite-level women's soccer was exceptionally high. Such an infrastructure so reliably supported was a vital influence on the flourishing of the game in the United States, as noted by general secretary of the federation, Hank Steinbrecher (see Box 8.1). This was not the case in many instances across the football landscape, where patriarchal biases kept women not just at the edge of the culture but out of the picture altogether.

FIFA to the rescue? 'A certain elegance'

FIFA's president João Havelange, 17 years into his presidency, eventually saw the potential for the development of the women's game when, in 1991, the Chinese Football Association hosted the first women's World Championship, prompting him to say that the 'first big step has been taken, thanks to the efficient Chinese organization and to twelve teams

> **Box 8.1: Women's soccer in the United States – 'ahead of the curve'**
>
> 'The reality is that in terms of [men's] football we have been behind the curve about 50 years; with women's football we are ahead of the curve and if we don't continually invest in the programme we are not going to be ahead of the curve for a long time. Forty-three percent of the registered players in the United States are female and in this country gender equity is not something you snicker about; it is something that is part of our social fabric now and we believe in it very, very strongly. Now was it the same commitment we made for the men, the answer is "No". It is not the same because they don't draw on the same kind of crowds on a regular basis. The future consumers of our product and our sponsors' products are women.'[4]

taking part, winners and losers alike, whose fairness, skill and efforts made this World Championship an unforgettable event'.[5] FIFA secretary general Blatter enthused on the quality of the Women's World Cup in Sweden in 1995, writing an editorial in *FIFA News* entitled 'The future is feminine'.[6] Reflecting on the event he described a women's game that is 'very alive, very well, and growing fast'. He emphasized 'positive features' which echoed the success of the inaugural event in China, 'notably the spirit of fair play, the will to attack, and the uninhibited enjoyment of the game', though was quick to observe that 'women's football is observing a style of its own', distinctive in its display of 'a certain elegance which has prevailed over a more robust impersonation of the man's game'.

Blatter expanded his analysis, noting that 'the better teams in Sweden were those whose players were true athletes, apparently capable of excelling in any sport', as opposed to 'those ... who were less athletically mobile'. The imagery is vivid here: gazelles and cart-horses come to mind. It's not the most sensitive of editorials as he sought to compliment the world's top women players and identify what he called 'a flavour all of its own' that 'will succeed in attracting players because of [women's football's] beauty and grace not because of its potential to mimic men players'.

But Blatter's commitment to a feminine football future looked less than convincing when encouraged by the Swiss newspaper *Sonntagsblick* in January 2004 to reveal his views on how FIFA might best increase the popularity of women's football:

> Let the women play in more feminine clothes like they do in volleyball. They could, for example, have tighter shorts. Female players are pretty, if you excuse me for saying so, and they already have some different rules to men – such as playing with a lighter ball. That decision was taken to create a more female aesthetic, so why not do it in fashion?[7]

Worldwide criticism poured in, many ridiculing his comments. Brandi Chastain, US footballer, Olympic gold-medal winner and world champion twice-over, told the *Los Angeles Times*: 'Anyone who thinks that a uniform will draw people to the game is seriously off base.'[8] She recalled and reflected upon the outcry later in the year in her book *It's Not About the Bra*.[9] There, she expressed her and her team-mates' 'irritation' at Blatter's implication that adding sex to 'sell our game' to promote interest would undermine the 'fact that we're good at it'; adding that 'it's ludicrous to talk about the size of our shorts, when there are so many bigger battles to fight in women's soccer, such as a global movement to create opportunity in the sport for all young girls'.

Blatter's FIFA did nevertheless open up unprecedented possibilities, expanding the reach, scale and profile of the women's game. At the pinnacle are FIFA's Women's World Cup, and the competitions/championships of each of the confederations.

Making the case

At a turn-of-the-century European Women and Sport Conference in Helsinki, Margaret Talbot observed that 'the most striking and universal difference between men and women in sport is in the organizations, bureaucracy and events management of sport, where men dominate positions of power, responsibility and decision-making'.[10] Talbot gets to the heart of the question here, particularly in relation to decision-making. Donna de Varona, who chaired the 1999 Women's World Cup, echoed her concerns, writing in 2004 of the need to sustain the momentum of the event, identifying three urgent actions: staging new and significant competitions; distributing prize money among World Cup squads; and designating women to 'leadership, officiating, management and coaching positions'.[11] She reflected as well on how the president and CEO of the US 1994 men's World Cup, Alan Rothenberg, 'was instrumental in making the 1999 Women's World Cup a model event for women's athletes', so ensuring that 'it can never again be doubted that women soccer players can attract interest, fill stadiums or earn high television ratings'.[12] It would be a rocky road towards the implementation of her recommended actions, but it cannot be denied that in most respects FIFA has delivered resources and funding that have made these goals achievable.

This outcome is attributable in large part to the strong profile of the women's game in the United States' wider sporting scene. 'With American football, baseball, basketball and ice hockey completely covering the male-dominated sports space of the United States, the women succeeded in a niche that remained unoccupied by the men.'[13]

The US women's success established a strong base on which FIFA could build as it further supported the development, and quality, of the women's game at the international level, including in the Olympic Games in which the football tournament is organized by FIFA. At the 2024 Paris Olympics the United States defeated Brazil in the tournament final at the Parc des Princes stadium in front of a sell-out crowd of women's football fans that was a celebration of the rising profile of the game. The Women's World Cup continues to expand this profile, with 32 teams in Brazil in 2027, and a bold, ambitious line-up of 48 teams for the 2031 edition in co-hosts Mexico and the United States, along with other members of the Confederation of North, Central America and Caribbean Association Football (CONCACAF). Women have begun to occupy positions of power within the FIFA administration, and have championed the development of the women's game. The FIFA Council requires that each confederation must be represented by at least one woman. FIFA staff numbers have increased dramatically since Gianni Infantino became president; a gender distribution of 60 per cent male to 40 per cent female with an age profile of 41 indicates a young and inclusive institutional profile, also representing 76 'first nationalities'.[14] Despite this gender balance, though, few women occupy the top positions in the FIFA hierarchy.

The grassroots

The elevated profile of women's football is anchored in the success of the big tournaments, which in turn are dependent upon the flow of talent upwards from the national football associations (NFAs), FIFA's core members. This means the players, referees, managers, coaches and administrators at all levels, and must include effective forms of connectivity with volunteers, enthusiasts and fans. FIFA's task in supporting this footballing infrastructure is a huge ask. At the very top level of the game the gap between the women and their male counterparts is vast. In 2019 Megan Rapinoe, US football star and LGBTQI+ activist, 'along with her US teammates sued their employers, the US National Soccer Federation, seeking equal pay with the men's team. In February 2022 the Federation agreed to a landmark $24 million agreement which will see tens of millions of dollars in back pay owed to female players'.[15]

In its 2023 financial report, FIFA headlined the women's game as a major priority for increased support and funding in the 2023–2026 financial cycle. If this can help close the gap with the men's game then all well and good, but it will be a long and demanding journey to get anywhere near the stratospheric salaries and bonuses of the male players.

FIFA's strategic objectives for 2023–2027 included (Goal 8) the 'FIFA Women's World Cup 2023™', and the event in Australia/New Zealand was undoubtedly an all-round success, establishing a momentum that should support the Brazil-based tournament in 2027 and an expanded format in 2031. In FIFA terms, though, this would be eclipsed by the 'FIFA World Cup 2026™' (Goal 9), labelled the 'Greatest show on the planet', and the 'Brand-new club competition' (Goal 10), the 'FIFA Club World Cup 2025'. Whatever the women's game was achieving, the men's game continued to be FIFA's primary priority.

Growing the women's game across the world has been a far from easy challenge for FIFA, deeply anchored as football has been and continues to be in male culture. In many cases NFAs have been slow and even reluctant to prioritize the development of women's football, and in numerous countries women have not been permitted to play the professional game. Multiple problems constrain the development of the women's game, as expressed by Chuka Onwumechili in Box 8.2.

Nevertheless, one positive outcome demonstrating the protest and resilience shown by women determined to play the game was achieved when Moroccan footballer Nouhaila Benzina became the first player to wear the Islamic headscarf at a top tournament.[16]

> **Box 8.2: Women's football in Africa – contending with multiple problems**
>
> 'There is also a religious divide. ... In most Muslim countries worldwide, girls and women are restricted from playing football because sports attire exposes their legs and hair and they become a focus for the male gaze. However ... girls have always resisted restrictions and found ways to participate.
>
> Funding represents another problem at all levels. Some countries fund women's national teams only for competitive matches but not for preparatory games. This means some teams rarely play.
>
> Other issues include homophobia and racism. Women players are often perceived to be lesbian and are discriminated against by both the public and football officials. This can have dire consequences. In South Africa, for example, a national team player, Eudy Simelane, was gang raped and murdered by men claiming to be 'cleansing' her from lesbianism.
>
> There is still a lot more work to do, to recruit more girls and grow women coaches. Public education is needed and the game needs funding for development.'[17]

Wearing a hijab in Morocco's defeat of South Korea at the 2023 World Cup has inspired young Muslim footballers in many countries to take up or keep playing the game: 'If I had seen someone like that [Benzina] when I was younger, it might have pushed me to play football at a younger age', said Asma Hassan, player at Saltley Stallions in Birmingham, England, one of the few clubs in the UK geared towards Muslim women. Hassan added that without such a role model she had in her earlier years felt that the game was essentially a male-dominated sport.

The hijab issue has proved a difficult challenge for FIFA, not least as there are several interpretations of the hijab itself.[18] In one, it is asserted that the hijab represents how 'bodies of Muslim women national players are the symbolic battlefield on which FIFA fights Muslims and Islam'. Politics and religion have constrained the development of the women's game. The Iranian Revolution in 1979 outlawed women's football, and it was a quarter of a century until it was revived in 2004. FIFA banned the hijab in 2007 and prevented Iran's women from playing an international match in 2011 when the team appeared wearing Islamic headscarves for its Summer Olympics qualifier against Jordan. This made Iran ineligible to qualify for the 2012 Summer Olympics.[19] The International Football Association Board (IFAB) – 'Guardians of the Laws of the Game' as it brands itself, comprising the four British football associations and four FIFA representatives[20] – announced the overturning of FIFA's ban the following year, the culmination of support from the United Nations, presidents of the African and Asian Football Confederation (AFC), and FIFA vice-president Prince Ali bin Al Hussein of Jordan, who travelled to London to lobby for the decision: 'I'm tackling this now because it is [a] big issue for many, many women all across the world.'[21]

As the Iranian international team was fighting its battles on the pitch, no women were looking on. They had been banned for decades from attending games, purportedly to protect them from hearing fans swear. In May 2018 President Infantino announced that Iranian president Hassan Rouhani had informed him of plans to allow women into the stadia soon. Later that year FIFA general secretary Fatma Samoura said that FIFA would work with Iran to make this breakthrough.[22] Iranian women – players' families, federation employees and relatives – had been allowed, earlier in October, to enter the Azadi Stadium in Tehran and watch a friendly soccer match between Iran and Bolivia. Eventually, one would hope, women from all levels of the game will be able to watch the match in the stadia, and play at all developmental levels to connect the grassroots to the battling footballers seeking to legitimate the game for all.

9
A LAW UNTO ITSELF?

FIFA and other sport governing bodies essentially make up the law under which they operate, arguing that they should be autonomous and free of oversight. This grants an extraordinary degree of independence to the organization, giving it the power to make decisions and judgements internally, disregarding conventional models of accountability and transparency expected of not-for-profit associations/institutions. Its autonomy rests upon a model of 'internal sports law' – its own disciplinary and judgemental investigations and procedures, alongside the independent, international Court of Arbitration for Sport – that should be respected by 'external sports law', this latter referring to established legal processes and procedures, particularly those of states.[1] In other words, 'hands off, we can handle it' is FIFA's unstated principle when it comes to matters of ethics and morality. Indeed, Stephen Weatherill sharply observes (see Box 9.1) that the likes of FIFA frequently

Box 9.1: What is 'sports law'? Do governing bodies in sport make law or are they merely subject to it?

'There are two kinds of "sports law". Call them internal and external. Internal sports law comprises the rules and practices according to which governing bodies structure their activities. In formal terms it is a system of private ordering, but it is remarkably dense and relatively sophisticated. Resonant "law-like" labels are used: there is an Olympic Charter, FIFA has its own governing "Statutes", World Athletics (formerly the IAAF) has a "Constitution". External sports law refers to the law of states and of international organizations such as the European Union which applies to sporting bodies when they operate within a particular jurisdiction. The thematic tension is generated by the typical claim of governing bodies in sport that they deserve autonomy from legal regulation – that is, that external sports law should respect the autonomy of internal sports law. In order to protect the integrity of their sport, they claim that their expertise in setting the rules of the game must be respected and that those rules should apply globally, free of fragmentation caused by compliance with the idiosyncracies of local law. They often claim too they are not really businesses at all, but rather custodians of social and cultural jewels. There are obvious normative questions about the proper scope that should be accorded to "sporting autonomy", but in practice many sports have been successful in creating their own dispute resolution system which keeps matters "in house". This is the province of arbitration, and the development of an intricate pattern of decisions taken by the Court of Arbitration for Sport.'[2]

present themselves not as 'businesses at all, but rather custodians of social and cultural jewels'.

Whose law is it anyway?

Weatherill offers a jargon-free description of the two dominant competing frameworks, enabling the lay reader to unravel the often impenetrable announcements of para-legal entities.

It is interesting to see how the legal world initially reacted, in the 1980s, to the emergence of the 'internal' sports law category. In Britain, for instance, Ken Foster, writing in 1993 on developments in 'sporting law', presented an illuminating vignette on the legal profession's view.[3] He identified 'an accelerating trend towards increased legal intervention in sport and a decline in the myth of sport as an autonomous and separate sphere where the law has no place'.[4] Further, he noted, this 'myth of sporting autonomy has been used as an argument against legal intervention in sport', as exemplified in 1986 in the words of British High Court Judge, and later law lord, Sir Nicolas Browne-Wilkinson: '[S]port would be better served if there was not running litigation at repeated intervals by people seeking to challenge the decisions of the ruling bodies.'[5] You can hear the authoritative and dismissive tone of the British elite here, the judge educated at Lancing College and Magdalen College, Oxford, emerging with a top-class degree in Jurisprudence. He was essentially sticking up for sport in his statement, uttering the words 'people seeking' with a sense of distaste for the seekers, and concluding with a headmasterly reminder that the 'ruling bodies' should make the decisions. But they were beginning not to make all of the decisions in that critical period when sport emerged as a new form of commodified spectacle, framed and underpinned by increasing levels of global commercialization; the 'people' continued to question the credibility of sport's decision-making processes. Foster commented on this too, noting that the 'explosion of litigation has been reflected in an increased interest by lawyers. Sports law is increasingly treated as a sub-division of the law'.[6] And the lawyers were indeed moving quickly into such spheres, as the International Amateur Athletics Federation (IAAF) learned when athlete Butch Reynolds, banned in 1990 for two years by the federation for testing positive for steroids, continued to dispute the ban throughout the following two decades. The governing body's position was crushingly inflexible as asserted by the IAAF's Arne Ljundqvist in the course of the litigation: '[W]e don't care in the least what [the civil courts] say; we have our rules and they are supreme.'[7] The arrogance in this and the over-confident sense of entitlement that spills from it are enough to stimulate generations of athletes and sportspersons to question the morality and authority of many governing bodies of sport, including of course FIFA.

Sepp Blatter frequently claimed that FIFA created a model of perfection in the ethical initiatives that were installed during his regime, in response to the allegations that had surfaced about FIFA finances and deal-making throughout the FIFA family. In September 2006 he welcomed former British athlete and Olympic gold medallist Sebastian Coe as FIFA's inaugural chair of the newly formed Ethics Committee.[8] Coe expressed his 'delight' in his selection for the position, confirmed his commitment to young people and sport, and emphasized that 'we must protect and support the ethics and morals of sport for future generations'. Sepp Blatter hailed Coe's 'total integrity' and insisted he would have 'total independence. To have someone from outside of football means he has no links with the football family and he has an ethical approach to sport'.[9] The new commission had no powers to deal with past cases, though, and Coe also joined the board of England's 2018 World Cup bid in February 2009, taking temporary leave of absence from his FIFA position.

This leave lasted for over a year, and in March 2010 Coe was replaced as chairman of FIFA's Ethics Committee. Maybe he saw the fireworks coming in December of that year at the conclusion of the contest for the 2018 and 2022 World Cups, and got out while his hands were still clean. New ethics chair Claudio Sulser, lawyer and former professional footballer, got the Ethics Committee to write to 'all member associations bidding for the 2018 and/or 2022 tournaments ... in order to remind them that they have signed regulations to respect fair play in this contest and that the Ethics Committee will remain vigilant to ensure that all regulations are adhered to'.[10]

Controversies surrounded the outcome of the bidding process for the 2018 (Russia) and 2022 (Qatar) events; Blatter and FIFA looked to rework the internal 'sport law' framework. Two separate chambers – 'investigatory' and 'adjudicatory' – were introduced in 2012, remaining in place to this day. Infantino was prominent in the group dealing with the fallout from the 2015 scandals and in 2018 his reforming FIFA published a promised 'new' ethics code. Two changes to the new code are revealing and concerning: first, 'forbidding' people bound by the code from making 'defamatory' statements about FIFA; second, closing potential investigation of any match-fixing offences, bribery and embezzlement by imposition of a statute of limitation whereby the issues 'may no longer be prosecuted after a lapse of 10 years'.[11] So crafty crooks need just to stick around for a decade to survive with impunity. We can only conclude that FIFA has consistently turned in on itself, shrouded by a culture of silence and survival. And, all along, it has been clear that the framework of a self-governing internal sports law is fragile and uncertain, as 'though it has a global governance function, FIFA is not equipped to conduct widespread, in-depth investigations'.[12] This simple judgement tears up the credibility of FIFA's juridical claims and pretensions.

Catching the crooks

No FIFA official or employee has ever served a jail sentence. Former secretary general Jérôme Valcke came close, seven years on from being dismissed, when the corruption allegations emerged in 2015. He was suspended in September, then sacked in January 2016. Six years later, convicted of forging documents and accepting bribes by a Swiss appeals court, he received an 11-month suspended prison sentence, along with a fine of CHF20,000.[13]

But, in the most dramatic of interventions, the FBI, the US Internal Revenue Service and the US Attorney (New York Eastern District) could, in 2015, identify criminal operations and so issue indictments on FIFA-related personnel when those operations/crimes were committed within the jurisdictional reach of US legal bodies. In this case the extensive malfeasance of FIFA-related officers and executives could lead to criminal charges and arrests on the basis of 'external sports law'. To see how the two 'sport law' frameworks have differed in tone and outcomes we now look, in the familiar context of the 2015 scandals, at two selected cases.[14]

Case 1: João Havelange

Hans-Joachim Eckert, chair of FIFA's Adjudicatory Chamber, referred in his report to the 'deliberately fraudulent and disloyal conduct' (in French *déloyal* means dishonest, underhand, unfair) that characterized the practices of ISL and FIFA, adding that

> it is certain that not inconsiderable amounts were channelled to former FIFA President Havelange and to his son-in-law Ricardo Texeira as well as to Dr. Nicolas Leoz, whereby there is no indication that any form of service was given in return by them. These payments were apparently made via front companies in order to cover up the true

recipient and are to be qualified as 'commissions', known today as 'bribes'. Known payments in this regard were made between 1992 and May 2000.[15]

Eckert also identified the flow of 'three-figure million sums' in Swiss francs and US dollars that 'were agreed upon as compensation for FIFA' in these transactions. Eckert emphasized that 'the acceptance of bribe money by Havelange, Teixeira and Leoz was not punishable under Swiss criminal law at that time', but also underlined that, as football officials, Havelange and Teixeira 'should not have accepted any bribe money', in essence damning

> the morally and ethically reproachable conduct of both persons ... President Blatter's conduct could not be classified in any way as misconduct with regard to any ethics rules ... [but] may have been clumsy because there could be an internal need for clarification, but this does not lead to any criminal or ethical misconduct.

Havelange's reputation had also been shredded the previous year when the Swiss Federal Court revealed that he 'received at least 1.5 million Swiss francs ($1.53 million) while Teixeira, who was at one time his son-in-law, was paid at least CHF 12.4 million ($12.64 million)'.[16]

Case 2: Chuck Blazer

Sealed proceedings from a New York (Brooklyn) court were filed on 3 June 2015, a few days after

Figure 9.1: Chuck Blazer

the scandals broke at the end of May. Blazer, seen in Figure 9.1 at his prime during the 1998 men's World Cup in Paris, pleaded guilty on all ten counts in the sealed proceedings, the first three of which pertained to his FIFA-based conspiracies over a period of 18 years. Count One:

> Beginning in or about 1993 and continuing through the early 2000s, I and others agreed to accept bribes and kickbacks in conjunction with the broadcast and the other rights to the 1996, 1998, 2000, 2002, and 2003 Gold Cups. Beginning in or around 2004 and continuing through 2011, I and others on the FIFA Executive Committee agreed to accept bribes in conjunction with the selection of South Africa as the host nation for the 2010 World Cup.

On Count Two Blazer described how, between 2004 and 2011, while still acting in his official capacity, he and other FIFA officials

> agreed to participate in a scheme to defraud FIFA and CONCACAF of the right to honest services by taking undisclosed bribes. I and others agreed to use e-mail, telephone, and a wire transfer into and out of the United States in furtherance of this scheme. Funds procured through these improper payments passed through JFK airport in the form of a check.

Count Three focused on the receipt of bribes and kickbacks from 2008 to 2011, involving the 'proceeds of an unlawful bribe' in which monies were moved between the United States and the Caribbean. Counts 4–9 covered income tax evasion; Count Ten referred to illegal financial arrangements in Blazer's name in the Bahamas, so 'violating the Federal Tax Law'.[17]

In these two extracts, one based on internal sport law, the second from the documentation of a criminal confession – an application of external sport law– there are substantial differences. Havelange was never interviewed and Eckert's adjudication clashed, at least interpretively, with the extensive and as yet unpublished report of the chair of the Investigative Chamber, US lawyer Michael Garcia. Blazer, in the second extract, is the star of the show, who has done a deal with the court to turn state's evidence, and pours out the detail of his astonishingly sustained and consistent career in collusion, corruption and criminality. The FBI and Inland Revenue Service cornered him in the end and, dying two years on, he was never sentenced, though in 2015 he had received a lifetime ban from FIFA. Havelange was clearly corrupt over long periods of time but protected, ironically, by the then lax Swiss criminal law. Tonally, these extracts read like they are from different universes: Eckert's Adjudicatory Chamber sounds like a wacky movie, a cross between a thriller and a heist; the Brooklyn US Courthouse conveys the chilly atmosphere of a crime movie.

For many observers, the time of internal sport law is up. Veteran human rights and social science scholar Helen Jefferson Lenskyj, who always has the International Olympic Committee (IOC) and often FIFA in her sights, has a clear perspective on the question of individual human rights of athletes: 'Instead of employing the *lex sportiva*/global sports law model, sport should follow best practice in international commercial arbitration. Mandatory arbitration clauses should be removed from contracts, and athletes should have recourse to national courts when arbitration fails to protect their human rights.'[18]

At the very least, FIFA could clarify the boundaries of its ethics framework, recognizing that its *lex sportiva* model is not suited to serious cases of individual or institutional criminality. FIFA's dual chamber system may be able to deal with ethical and moral issues arising from forms of dodgy collaboration or exploitative collusion. But tackling the often-embedded practices of corruption and explicit criminality in the football world must surely be the business of external sports law. FIFA began life as a rule-maker and a regulator, arbiter of an emerging international football culture and product that could be understood and shared by all. This is really what FIFA was for, though its escalating profile and ambitions have for the most part clouded these foundational and fundamental principles.

10
CONCLUSION

FIFA was formed as essentially a diplomatic initiative to enable international football teams to play against each other with a shared understanding of the rules. This brought an awareness of the agreed Laws of the Game to encounters that previously had often boiled over as teams sought to play by their own traditional rules. The Football Association of England, formed 41 years before FIFA, had developed influential models of the rules and initially snubbed approaches from the European creators of a world governing body that would oversee fixtures between international sides. By 1930, these included a global competition that over the next century would rival the Summer Olympics as the world's most dazzling sporting spectacle.

In this sense the answer to our question *What Is FIFA For?* is simple and straightforward: it was founded as an international body with a mission to take modern football to countries across the world. Its reach was of course initially limited due to cultural, political and economic differences, the constraints of international travel and its concentration on the men's game. But once it existed, even the stubborn English Football Association (FA) had to recognize its relevance, providing a second FIFA president, who from 1906 guided FIFA's development and held things together until his death in 1918.

Survival after the First World War, the growing membership of FIFA and its contribution to the football tournaments of the Olympic Games sustained its international profile and the staging of the inaugural World Cup in 1930 in Uruguay consolidated its presence as a credible international operation. We have here another answer to our question *What Is FIFA For?* It is for the good of the game, crossing international boundaries and bringing together culturally distinct and politically varied nations and peoples. As the World Cup became bigger and a firm fixture in global calendars, FIFA could claim that it was here to stay, and moved its base to Switzerland in 1932, registering itself as a non-commercial organization, a not-for-profit body whose income should be reinvested for the benefits of the organization itself.

For much of the 20th century FIFA chugged along and football fans, spectators and players had little awareness of the nature of the organization. There was a somewhat esoteric aura around its small-scale operation in its modest setting in Zurich, but within its expanding networks, political interests were becoming explicit and geopolitical blocs were emerging to seek influence and power. A FIFA based in Switzerland and dominated by Europeans supported World Cup events in the 1930s at which Italy's national team, strongly backed by Fascist Benito Mussolini, triumphed twice in a row, in Rome in 1934 and – see Figure 10.1 – at its French host's event in Paris in 1938. Following Uruguay's triumph on home soil in 1930 this established a rivalry between European football and its South American counterparts that would fuel interest for the international game for the foreseeable future. No team outside Europe or South America has won the men's World Cup. So here we have a third answer to *What Is FIFA For?* It is, one could argue in sympathy with football lovers across Africa, Asia, North and Central Americas/Caribbean, and Oceania, for the established giants of the game, especially those who have been there from the beginning. Let the emerging teams across the continental confederations (CCs) have a bit of action, but for the most part the elite European and South American sides will emerge once more as the main challengers; only England and Spain have won the men's World Cup just once. For almost a century this dominance has defined the event.

For fans of the football elite, there has been much to enjoy. In a way we can see the answer to a tweaked question here: *Who Is FIFA For?* It is for the expanding audiences – both live and onscreen – that keep the global supershow on the road. And there is an air of excitement, if not expectation, in the growing numbers of competitors at the 2026 World Cup. If Morocco can get as far as it did in Qatar in 2022, or as South Korea

CONCLUSION

Figure 10.1: France 1938 – foot firmly on the ball, but Italy wins its second World Cup

did in Seoul in 2002 – both reaching a semi-final – and go one better to reach the final itself in the United States, the Euro/South American dominance will be broken. FIFA's aspirations to grow the professional game across the world would be achieved on the pitch itself, shared by world-breaking levels of screen-based fans.

Away from the highlights of the World Cup, there are issues that FIFA has begun to face. We have seen examples in global football development of persisting forms of corruption, and Gianni Infantino has also acknowledged the problem of match manipulation, saying at the First FIFA Integrity Summit in Singapore in 2024 that '[n]obody is immune from this threat ... as a multi-billion dollar industry, football would always be a tempting target for criminal activity'.[1] Much needs to be uncovered on the nature of match manipulation and match-fixing. Human rights activists have, with more success, reported on the issue of women's rights in numerous cases as well as the exploitative conditions which immigrant workers have been forced to endure when building football stadia. FIFA has shown some concern about such rights, but fails to convince us of its commitment to defend them. FIFA *should* be for and in support of the rights of all involved in the game, from grassroots to the professional elite; yet in March 2021 FIFA dissolved its human rights advisory board set up in 2017.

FIFA's relationships with its member associations and its commercial stakeholders may look strong and robust but in practice are pragmatic and weak. On 27 May 2025 – a decade on from the arrests of senior officials at the Baur au Lac hotel in Zurich which ignited the fires that became perhaps the biggest worldwide scandal in the history of sport – the human rights group FairSquare reaffirmed the core issue; at the heart of FIFA's governance problems there is a continuing 'deeply problematic power dynamic between the organization's executive branch and its member associations'. In short, we have seen that a model of patronage allows FIFA to buy the loyalty and allegiance of national football associations (NFAs); ethical principles are sidelined despite the reforms announced in 2016.

FIFA's corporate stakeholders in the sport marketing and broadcasting fields have also tended to stay silent throughout controversy and crisis, with their focus on profits rather than principles. Throughout the decade following the 2015 scandals, FIFA's president Gianni Infantino has assumed the role of an executive president, reducing forms of consultation, bypassing the FIFA Council and announcing decisions in ways contrary to the FIFA statutes. He has enhanced his status and his reputation as a dynamic decision-maker but at the expense of the credibility of the FIFA organizational infrastructure that he put into place.

Why does all this matter then? There is always hope, and hope can be projected into a future in which FIFA engages with its stakeholders more openly and explicitly, considering ways in which its deep resources can be used to strengthen the base of the football pyramid and engage with football at all levels. FIFA could ensure that in all its member associations'

(NFAs') actions and interventions are consistently implemented, thereby bringing some genuine element of reality to bear upon its notion of 'the whole football community'. In some ways FIFA is more buoyant than it has ever been, running numerous international projects. In 2023, for example, it set up 'a 50% interest in Football Development Ventures Ltd, a company located in Kigali, Rwanda, that manage and operate the African Football League'.[2] And it continues to subsidize football developments and schemes in the NFAs, its member associations, to the tune of 'up to USD 8 million for the four-year cycle (2023–2026)' for each association.

Some FIFA initiatives have without doubt generated progressive change, in particular in the women's game. The professional football world has nevertheless been slow to invest in the expansion of women's leagues and the infrastructure of the women's game. The 'total media engagement' figures for the 2023 event in Australia and New Zealand – made up of linear TV, digital/streaming, social media and FIFA platforms – topped two billion. Revenues generated from these sources should be fairly and generously redistributed across the women's game to underpin the game's continuing development in Brazil in 2027, the United States in 2031 and, in its expanded 48-team format, in the UK in 2035.

Fifpro, the International Federation of Professional Footballers, welcomed in principle the FIFA announcement of the expansion for 2035 but emphasized that inclusive decision-making and cooperative planning would be essential to support the expansion; and added that such a global expansion must go hand-in-hand with 'improved labour conditions and the advancement of players', along with development for the women's game further down the pyramid. 'This is the only path to true sustainability, expansion and progress', Fifpro reminded the football world.

Currently, FIFA needs football more than football needs FIFA. CCs could go their own way at almost any moment. That is why FIFA must begin to show more transparently and with genuine accountability just what, and for whom, FIFA *is* for – the players, the fans, the communities from which talented players emerge. Splits in the international sporting world *do* occur – cricket in the 1970s, boxing seemingly incessantly – and football is not immune to such threats. There remains much to be done.

In particular, FIFA needs to justify how what began as a 'normal association' with 'just the same status as a yodelling association in a mountain village', as Swiss parliamentarian Roland Buechel put it in May 2015, has morphed into a global behemoth. He is emphatic that 'this is not the correct way to be registered for a billion dollar company'. It also remains anomalous, to many general sports fans as well as football followers, that such an organization can be permitted to live by its own rules. Statutes drawn up initially in Paris in 1904 still provide the format for the operation of the organization, and can in their expanded and modern-day form lay down the law – literally – because it has set up a whole legalistic infrastructure that works just for the organization, with no accountability to state-based legal systems and jurisdictions.

If FIFA does not address the many questions that have been raised repeatedly in recent years, continuing to hide behind its internal statutes and rulebooks, camouflaged by the glory of the spectacle and the silky communication skills of the social media, the football world may begin to look away. The question might then be further tweaked: *What Was FIFA For?* But for FIFA to thrive with integrity, we must continue to ask the questions, to unmute the voices of supine FIFA personnel and stakeholders alike; in short, to act.

NOTES

Chapter 1

1. Alexandra Topping, 'History, memory, grief and belonging: My bittersweet Goodison farewell', *The Observer*, 9 February 2025, p. 14.
2. Felipe Cardenas, 'Greenland, out in the cold and in geopolitical crosshairs, sees hope in Concacaf', *The Athletic*, 18 February 2025.
3. FIFA Forward, *Regulations: FIFA Forward Development Programme (Forward 3.0)*, December 2022, p. 4.
4. Theodor W. Adorno, *Prisms* (Neville Spearman, 1967), p. 81.
5. Adorno's approach to sport, as William Morgan sees it, 'molds human beings to the machine' and can also serve as a 'model for totalitarian mass rallies'. See William J. Morgan, 'Adorno on sport: The case of the fractured dialectic', *Theory & Society* 17:6 (1988), pp. 813–838, at p. 818. In my own interpretation, FIFA's grip on the global sport spectacle offers more open-ended possibilities than this even within the realm of unfreedom.
6. Pierre Bourdieu, *Practical Reason: On the Theory of Action* (Stanford University Press, 1998), p. 145.
7. It is not my intent to provide a comprehensive cultural, social and economic account of football; for that, I recommend that readers become familiar with the comprehensive and insightful works of David Goldblatt. See David Goldblatt, *The Ball is Round: A Global History of Soccer* (Penguin/Riverhead Books, 2008) and *The Age of Football: The Global Game in the Twenty-First Century* (Macmillan, 2019).

Chapter 2

1. FIFA, *The Football Landscape: Making Football Truly Global*, https://publications.fifa.com/en/vision-report-2021/the-football-landscape/, accessed 30 January 2025.
2. Deloitte Football Money League 2025, *Analysis*, 23 January 2025, https://www.deloitte.com/uk/en/services/financial-advisory/analysis/deloitte-football-money-league.html?icid=learn_more_content_click, accessed 18 April 2025.

3   Pierre Lanfranchi, Christiane Eisenberg, Tony Mason and Alfred Wahl, *100 Years of Football: The FIFA Centennial Book* (Weidenfeld & Nicolson, 2004), p. 12.
4   Ramsey Fahs, 'A $22 million soccer museum in China makes claim as the "birthplace of football"', *The China Project*, 14 March 2019, https://thechinaproject.com/2019/03/14/linzi-football-museum-china-as-birthplace-of-football/, accessed 30 January 2025.
5   David Goldblatt, *The Ball is Round: A Global History of Soccer* (Penguin/Riverhead Books, 2008), p. 5.
6   Ibid, p. 18.
7   Stanley Rous and Donald Ford, *A History of the Laws of Association Football* (Fédération Internationale de Football Association, 1974), pp. 9–11.
8   *The Comedy of Errors* included a reference to the game, in the words of Dromio of Ephesus: 'Am I so round with you as you with me, That like a football you do spurn me thus?'; the context here is the theme of being maltreated, kicked about as if you are no more than a football. And in *King Lear*, Goneril's steward Oswald is insulted by the Earl of Kent saying to Lear, 'I'll not be strucken, my lord'; Kent's response, 'Nor tripped neither, you base football player', is undoubtedly locating Oswald in among the low-life. In both examples football denotes low status and rough play, if not riotous excess. Jonathan Bate and Eric Rasmussen (eds) *William Shakespeare, Complete Works* (Macmillan, 2007), p. 225, Act 2, Scene 1, lines 80/81, *The Comedy of Errors*; and p. 2,021, Act 1, Scene 4, lines 67/88, *King Lear*.
9   Rous and Ford, *A History*, p. 9.
10 John Simkin, 'The encyclopedia of British football: Football rules', *Sparticus Educational*, September 1997 (updated January 2020), https://spartacus-educational.com/Frules.htm, accessed 27 April 2025.
11 Melvyn Bragg, 'Introduction', in *The Rules of Association Football 1863* (Bodleian Library, 2006), p. 14.
12 Ibid, pp. 14–15.
13 Mike Huggins, 'Preface: An original, important and seminal work', in J.A. Mangan and Colm Hickey, *Soccer's Missing Men: Schoolteachers and the Spread of Association Football* (Routledge, 2009), p. xviii.
14 Adrian Harvey, *Football: The First Hundred Years – the Untold Story* (Routledge, 2005), p. 62.
15 Richard Giulianotti, *Football: A Sociology of the Global Game* (Polity Press, 1999), p. 5.
16 Harvey, *Football*, p. 69.
17 Ibid, p. 233.
18 Lanfranchi et al, *100 Years*, pp. 19–21.

NOTES

19 Dave Russell, 'From evil to expedient: The legalization of professionalism in English football, 1884–85', in Stephen Wagg (ed) *Myths and Milestones in the History of Sport* (Palgrave Macmillan, 2011), pp 32–56, at p. 32.
20 FIFA Museum, 'Scotland v. England: 150 years of international football', https://www.fifamuseum.com/en/explore/fifamuseumplus/blog/Scotland-v-England-1, accessed 18 April 2025.
21 Miguel Galan, Paulo C. Godov and Joseph S. Blatter, *Football History, Laws of the Game, Referees* (FIFA, 1986), p. 4.
22 FIFA Museum, 'Scotland v. England'.
23 This sub-section draws in parts on three of the author's publications: Alan Tomlinson, 'FIFA: Beginnings, tensions, trajectories', in Stefan Rinke and Kay Schiller (eds) *The FIFA World Cup 1930–2010: Politics, Commerce, Spectacle and Identities* (Wallstein Verlag, 2014), pp. 30–46; (with E.A. Brett), 'Mis-governing world football: Agency and (non)accountability at FIFA', *Oxford Journal of Legal Studies*, 45:1 (Spring 2025), pp. 108–137; and 'Global sports governance and politics: Learning from the FIFA story', in Joseph Maguire, Mark Falcous and Katie Liston (eds) *The Business and Culture of Sports: Society, Politics, Economy, Environment*, Vol. 4 (Macmillan, 2019), pp. 77–89. Examples discussed here are taken from Harvey, *Football*, pp. 233–241.
24 FIFA Museum, 'From Leipzig to Paris: The story of how the DFB became the first association to join FIFA', https://www.fifamuseum.com/en/explore/fifamuseumplus/blog/From-Leipzig-to-Pari, accessed 27 April 2025.
25 Tomlinson, 'Global sports governance', pp. 78–79.
26 Lanfranchi et al, *100 Years*, pp. 64 and 68.
27 Ibid, p. 64.
28 Alan Tomlinson, *Sir Stanley Rous and the Growth of World Football: An Englishman Abroad* (Cambridge Scholars Publishing, 2020).
29 Personal communication, 29 October 1996.
30 Heidi Blake and Jonathon Calvert, *The Ugly Game: The Qatari Plot to Buy the World Cup* (Simon & Schuster, 2015), p. 3.
31 Office of Public Affairs/U.S. Department of Justice (2015) 'Webb et al, Indictment 15 CR 0252 (RJD) (RML)', 20 May 2015, 89–94, direct quote from para 218.
32 Andrew Jennings, *Foul: The Secret World of FIFA: Bribes, Vote Rigging and Ticket Scandals* (HarperSport, 2006) narrates numerous stories and cases of corrupt networks in FIFA and across the confederations during the early years of Blatter's presidency.
33 United States District Court Eastern District of New York, *United States of America Against Charles Gordon Blazer Defendant* 13-CR-602

(RJD), 13-MC-1011, US Courthouse, Brooklyn New York, Sealed Proceeding, 25 November 2013 10a.m. Original Document (pdf).
34 Alan Tomlinson, 'Blazing a trial', *When Saturday Comes* 341 (July 2015), p. 16.
35 Alan Tomlinson, *FIFA: The Men, the Myths and the Money* (Routledge, 2014), pp. 145–146.
36 Bombreport, *United Passions*, https://bombreport.com/yearly-breakdowns/2015-2/united-passions/, accessed 10 July 2025.
37 Jordan Hoffman, '*United Passions* review – FIFA propaganda is pure cinematic excrement', *The Guardian*, 4 June 2015.
38 Andy Edwards, 'After three presidents indicted, CONCACAF to lead by committee', *nbcsports.com*, 7 December 2015.
39 'Nine FIFA officials and five corporate executives indicted for racketeering conspiracy and corruption', Press Release, 27 May 2015, Office of Public Affairs, U.S. Department of Justice (Archives).
40 Office of Public Affairs/U.S. Department of Justice (2015) 'Webb et al, Indictment 15 CR 0252 (RJD) (RML)', para 39.
41 Murad Ahmed, John Sugden and Alan Tomlinson, 'João Havelange, world football chief, 1916–2016: FIFA president who became tainted by bribery findings', *Financial Times*, 16 August 2016, https://www.ft.com/content/8d45ab96-349c-11e6-bda0-04585c31b153, accessed 15 March 2025.

Chapter 3

1 Keir Radnege, 'The evolution of "national" teams', *World Soccer*, December 2024, p. 14.
2 FIFA, 'Around FIFA: Professional football', https://publications.fifa.com/en/annual-report-2021/around-fifa/professional-football-2021/, accessed 5 March 2025.
3 Personal interview, 27 November 1996.
4 CONCACAF, 'Member associations', https://www.concacaf.com/inside-concacaf/member-associations/, accessed 12 February 2025.
5 InsideFIFA, 'Division: Member associations', https://inside.fifa.com/en/organisation/divisions/member-associations, accessed 8 May 2025.
6 InsideFIFA, 'FIFA president visits FIFA Forward development projects in Vanuatu', https://inside.fifa.com/organisation/president/news/fifa-president-visits-fifa-forward-development-projects-in-vanuatu, accessed 6 May 2025.
7 Kieron O'Connor, 'Donald Trump eyes $50bn boost from 2026 FIFA World Cup', insidersport.com, 7 May 2025, https://insidersport.com/2025/05/07/donald-trump-2026-fifa-world-cup/, accessed 3 July 2025.

NOTES

8   InsideFIFA, 'UEFA', https://inside.fifa.com/associations/UEFA, accessed 7 March 2025.
9   Samindra Kuntri, 'Russia's soccer ban: Could UEFA and FIFA lift the suspension?', *Forbes Daily*, 28 February 2025, https://www.forbes.com/sites/samindrakunti/2025/02/28/russias-soccer-ban-could-uefa-and-fifa-lift-the-suspension/, accessed 7 March 2025.
10 FIFA, *FIFA Statutes, May 2022 edition*, pp. 17 and 26, https://digitalhub.fifa.com/m/3815fa68bd9f4ad8/original/FIFA_Statutes_2022-EN.pdf, accessed 8 February 2024.
11 Joshua Kloke, 'This is soccer in Greenland: potentially CONCACAF's newest member: "I think we are ready" ', *The Athletic*, 31 May 2024; and Felipe Cardenas, 'Greenland, out in the cold and in geo-political crosshairs, sees hope in CONCACAF,' *The Athletic*, 18 February 2025.
12 InsideFIFA, 'Say no to racism: My game is fair play', https://inside.fifa.com/tournaments/mens/confederationscup/russia2017/watch/fifa-say-no-to-racism-my-game-is-fair-play-2895097, accessed 12 July 2025.
13 BBC Sport, 'FIFA proposes five-pillar plan to combat racism', 16 May 2024, https://www.bbc.co.uk/sport/football/articles/cv2r2yvye05o, accessed 12 July 2025.
14 Ben Carrington, *Race, Sport and Politics: The Sporting Black Diaspora* (SAGE, 2010), p. 164.
15 InsideFIFA, 'FIFA Forward core principles: Financial entitlements', https://inside.fifa.com/advancing-football/fifa-forward/core-principles, accessed 25 July 2025.

Chapter 4

1   Susan Strange, *Casino Capitalism* (Manchester University Press, 1997), pp. vi–vii.
2   Robert K. Barney, Stephen R. Wenn and Scott G. Martyn, *Selling the Five Rings: The International Olympic Committee and the Rise of Olympic Commercialism* (University of Utah Press, 2002), p. 87.
3   Ibid, p. 88.
4   Alan Tomlinson, 'The supreme leader sails on: Leadership, ethics and governance in FIFA', *Sport in Society* 17:9 (2014), pp. 1155–1169, at p. 1158.
5   Alan Tomlinson, 'The making of the global sports economy: ISL, Adidas and the rise of the corporate player in world sport', in Michael L. Silk, David L. Andrews and C.L. Cole (eds), *Sport and Corporate Nationalisms* (Berg, 2005), pp. 35–65, at p. 42. Further quotes from Nally are from interview transcripts (in possession of author), provided by the late Andrew Jennings.

6 'Albert Killeen obituary – family-placed death notice', *The Atlanta Journal-Constitution*, 20 October 2004, https://www.legacy.com/us/obituaries/atlanta/name/albert-killeen-obituary?id=29800298, accessed 15 May 2025.
7 Tomlinson, 'The making of the global sports economy', p. 42.
8 Barney et al, *Selling the Five Rings*, p. 174.
9 Neil Wilson, *The Sports Business* (Mandarin, 1988), p. 182.
10 Tomlinson, 'The making of the global sports economy', p. 55.
11 David Conn, *The Fall of the House of FIFA* (Yellow Jersey Press, 2017), p. 150. Conn's chapter 10, 'Bribery in Switzerland is not a crime', dissects several key documents and reports in his revelation of the embedded corrupt and criminal practices of FIFA personnel and of FIFA itself as a governing body granted non-profit status and committed to charitable principles.
12 Alan Tomlinson, *FIFA: The Men, the Myths and the Money* (Routledge, 2014), p. 3.
13 Andrew Jennings, 'FIFA: An era of corruption nears its end', presentation at *Play the Game* conference, 2007, pp 1–2, https://www.playthegame.org/media/zcjdg0eq/jennings-paper-2007.pdf, accessed 14 March 2025.
14 Jakob Staun, 'The fall of ISL', *Play the Game*, 2 June 2006, https://www.playthegame.org/news/the-fall-of-isl/, accessed 14 March 2025.
15 Jakob Staun, 'What FIFA lost on ISL', *Play the Game*, 2 June 2006, https://www.playthegame.org/news/what-fifa-lost-on-isl/, accessed 11 May 2025.
16 Bei Bei She, 'FIFA plans bonds to insure World Cup', Rediff.com, 1 September 2023, https://www.rediff.com/sports/2003/sep/01fifa.htm, accessed 11 May 2025.
17 FIFA press release, 'FIFA concludes securitization with Credit Suisse', https://www.sportcal.com/pressreleases/fifa-concludes-securitisation-with-credit-suisse/, accessed 16 March 2025.
18 Daniela Sirtori-Cortina, 'Credit Suisse slammed for AML failings linked to FIFA corruption', *CitywireAmericas*, 18 September 2018, https://citywire.com/americas/news/credit-suisse-slammed-for-aml-failings-linked-to-fifa-corruption/a1156356, accessed 16 March 2025.
19 Alan Tomlinson, 'Global sports governance and politics: Learning from the FIFA story', in Joseph Maguire, Mark Falcous and Katie Liston (eds) *The Business and Culture of Sports: Society, Politics, Economy, Environment*, Vol. 4 (Macmillan, 2019), pp. 78–89, at p. 82.
20 David Goldblatt, 'Another kind of history: Globalization, global history and the World Cup', in Stefan Rinke and Kay Schiller (eds) *The FIFA*

NOTES

World Cup 1930–2010: Politics, Commerce, Spectacle and Identities (Wallstein Verlag, 2014), pp. 15–29, at p. 19.

21 Stefan Rinke, 'Globalizing football in times of crisis: The first World Cup in Uruguay in 1930', in Stefan Rinke and Kay Schiller (eds) *The FIFA World Cup 1930–2010: Politics, Commerce, Spectacle and Identities* (Wallstein Verlag, 2014), pp. 49–65, at p. 59.

22 Paul MacInnes, 'FIFA will consider expanding World Cup to 64 teams for 2030 tournament', *The Guardian*, 6 March 2025.

23 The figures for the 1998–2022 spectator numbers are from Statista, 'Average and total attendance at FIFA football World Cup games from 1930–2018', https://www.statista.com/, accessed 24 June 2025; and FIFA, 'FIFA World Cup Qatar 2022™ in numbers', https://publications.fifa.com/en/annual-report-2022/tournaments-and-events/fifa-world-cup-quatar-2022/fifa-world-cup-qatar-2022-in-numbers/, accessed 24 June 2025.

24 Figures on spectator and match numbers for the 1930–1994 World Cups are a gift from FIFA's Public Relations department, in the form of posters-cum-cards containing images and data referring to all World Cups over that period. These were received at a FIFA-supported event, 'The Relevance and Impact of FIFA World Cups, 1930–2010', held in April 2013 at the home of FIFA in Zurich. The editors of the book that emerged from that event noted and appreciated 'FIFA's willingness to facilitate such a free exchange of opinions and its readiness to listen to critical remarks' (see Stefan Rinke and Kay Schiller (eds) *The FIFA World Cup 1930–2010: Politics, Commerce, Spectacle and Identities* (Wallstein Verlag, 2014), p. 11). I echo the editors' appreciation of this openness and, as one of the presenters, reaffirm that 'the scholars contributing to' the international conference were in no way 'restricted in their views on the World Cup'.

25 FIFA, 'A look ahead to 2023–2026', *Annual Report 2022*, https://publications.fifa.com/en/annual-report-2022/finances/2023-2026-cycle-budget-and-2024-detailed-budget/, accessed 6 March 2025

26 FIFA, *FIFA World Cup 26™ Media Partners*, https://digitalhub.fifa.com/m/af2cdbbd380d70c/original/FWC26-Media-Rights-Licensees-Overview.pdf, accessed 6 March 2025.

27 InsideFIFA, 'Partners', https://inside.fifa.com/tournament-organisation/partners, accessed 17 March 2025.

28 Tomlinson, *FIFA: The Men, the Myths and the Money*, p. 142.

29 Ibid, p. 143. MasterCard was the plaintiff in a legal action, *MasterCard International Incorporated v. Fédération Internationale de Football Association*, 7 December 2006, Note 26, p. 147.

30 Richard Gruneau, *Sport and Modernity* (Polity, 2017), p. 187.

Chapter 5

1. John G. Ruggie, *For the Game. For the World: FIFA & Human Rights – Corporate Responsibility Initiative Report No. 68* (Harvard Kennedy School, 2016), p. 36.
2. Andrew Jennings, *The Dirty Game: Uncovering the Scandal at FIFA* (Century, 2015).
3. Ibid, p. 247. Further quotes on this case are from the same chapter, 'Blatter rewrites his ethics code'.
4. Bonita Mersiades, *Whatever it Takes: The Inside Story of the FIFA Way* (Powderhouse Press, 2018), p. 3.
5. Ibid, p. 228.
6. Ibid.
7. FIFA, 'Objective 3', FIFA Statutes, FIFA Legal Handbook, September Edition 2024, p. 13, https://www.acerislaw.com/wp-content/uploads/2024/10/24-FIFA-Legal-Handbook-Reduced-Size.pdf
8. Ibid, 'Objective 2a', p. 12.
9. Nicholas McGeehan, Usman Jawed and Marilyn Croser, *Substitute: The Case for External Reform at FIFA* (FairSquare/fairsq.org, 2024), pp. 1–177.
10. Ibid, p. 17.
11. Alan Tomlinson, 'No contest', *When Saturday Comes* 437 (December 2023), p. 32.
12. FIFA, *FIFA World Cup 2030™ Bid Evaluation Report* (FIFA, 2004), p. 10.
13. FIFA, *FIFA World Cup 2034™ Bid Evaluation Report* (FIFA, 2024), p. 5.
14. Ibid, p. 5.
15. Jonathan Wilson, 'FIFA's Infantino and Saudi Arabia 1, football and human decency 0', *The Guardian/Observer*, 8 December 2024, https://www.theguardian.com/football/blog/2024/dec/07/fifa-infantino-saudi-arabia-world-cup-2034, accessed 9 December 2024.
16. Pete Pattisson, 'Saudi's World Cup bid victory is crushing defeat for migrant workers' rights', *The Guardian/Observer*, 8 December 2024.
17. Sports and Rights Alliance and Amnesty International, *High Stakes Bids: Dangerously Flawed Human Rights Strategies for the 2030 and 2034 FIFA World Cups* (Amnesty International Ltd., 2024), p. 4.
18. Ibid, pp. 24 and 25.
19. McGeehan et al, *Substitute*, p. 134.
20. Alan Tomlinson, 'FIFA: "For the game. For the world"?: The world governing body's escalating crisis of credibility', in Alan Bairner, John Kelly and Jung Woo Lee (eds) *Routledge Handbook of Sport and Politics* (Routledge, 2018), pp. 251–265.
21. Ibid, p. 258.

22 Ibid, p. 259.
23 David Goldblatt, *The Age of Football: The Global Game in the Twenty-First Century* (Macmillan, 2019), p. 552.
24 Ibid, p. 549.
25 Bassil Mikdadi, 'Aspirational wealth: Qatar', *When Saturday Comes* 358 (December 2016), p. 8.
26 Ibid, p. 149.
27 Klas Lundström, 'Argentina's blood-stained 1978 World Cup', *Tribune*, 2 December 2022, https://tribunemag.co.uk/2022/12/argentinas-blood-stained-1978-world-cup, accessed 18 June 2025.
28 Personal communication, 22 May 2025.

Chapter 6

1 Bill Murray, *Football: A History of the World Game* (Scolar Press, 1994), p. 115.
2 Guy Oliver, *The Guinness Book of World Soccer: The History of the Game in Over 150 Countries*, 2nd edition (Guinness Publishing, 1995), p. 634.
3 Peter Beck, *Scoring for Britain: International Football and International Politics, 1900–1939* (Frank Cass, 1999), p. 259.
4 Murray, *Football*, p. 115.
5 FIFA, *Minutes of 6th Annual FIFA Congress*, Budapest, 30–31 May 1909, in Beck, *Scoring for Britain*, pp. 50–51.
6 InsideFIFA, 'CONMEBOL', https://inside.fifa.com/associations/CONMEBOL, accessed 23 February 2025.
7 Tim Vickery, 'South America: 2025 Club World Cup preview', *World Soccer*, June 2025, p. 59.
8 John Sugden and Alan Tomlinson, *FIFA and the Contest for World Football: Who Rules the Peoples' Game?* (Polity Press, 1998), pp. 203–204.
9 Jack Anderson, 'Prosecuting sports corruption is tough, and we should look to another solution', *The Conversation*, 19 June 2015, https://theconversation.com/prosecuting-sports-corruption-is-tough-and-we-should-look-to-another-solution-43554, accessed 26 June 2025.
10 Ed Farnsworth, 'The origins of soccer in Philadelphia, part 5: Local college-based football after the 1863 Laws of the Game', *College Soccer*, 16 April 2020 (Society for American Soccer History), https://www.ussoccerhistory.org/the-origins-of-soccer-in-philadelphia-part-5-local-college-based-football-after-the-1863-laws-of-the-game/, accessed 20 January 2025.

11 Andrei S. Markovits, 'The other "American exceptionalism": Why is there no soccer in the United States?', *Praxis International* 8, Issue 2 (1988), pp. 125–150, at p. 125.
12 Rothenberg was speaking to M. Palmer of *The Sunday Telegraph Review*, see John Sugden and Alan Tomlinson, 'What's left when the circus leaves town? An evaluation of World Cup USA 1994', *Sociology of Sport Journal* 13 (1996), pp. 238–258, at p. 246.
13 Brian Glanville is quoted in ibid, p. 254.
14 Jon Arnold, 'Turning 30 – Major League Soccer', *World Soccer*, March 2025, p. 40.
15 Ibid, p. 43.
16 Ibid, p. 40.
17 Andrew Crawford, 'Force major', *When Saturday Comes* 452 (April 2025), p. 26.
18 CONCACAF, 'Infantino: "New CONCACAF HQ represents new chapter of football in region"', 19 November 2018, https://www.concacaf.com/en/news/infantino-new-concacaf-hq-represents-new-chapter-of-football-in-region/, accessed 20 December 2024.
19 Michelle Kaufman, 'FIFA Legal and Compliance Division working full-time out of new Coral Gables office', *Miami Herald*, 5 September 2024, https://sports.yahoo.com/fifa-legal-compliance-division-working-191114093.html, accessed 20 January 2025.
20 Paul Nicholson, 'FIFA paying Miami school fees for its $4.67m president's daughter', *Inside World Football*, 11 December 2024, https://www.insideworldfootball.com/2024/12/11/fifa-paying-miami-school-fees-4-67m-presidents-daughter/, accessed 4 January 2025.
21 Adam S. Beissel and David L. Andrews, 'Art of the deal: Donald Trump, the 2026 FIFA Men's World Cup, and the geo-politics of football aspiration', in Bryan C. Clift and Alan Tomlinson (eds) *Populism in Sport, Leisure and Popular Culture* (Routledge, 2021), pp. 234–253, at p. 240.
22 Ibid, p. 246.
23 Ibid, p. 237.

Chapter 7

1 Patrick Barclay, 'Continental drift a long time coming for Africa', *The Times*, 6 January 2010.
2 Stanley Rous, 'Foreword', in Maurice Golesworthy ('compiled by'), *The Encyclopaedia of Association Football Sixth Edition* (The Sportsmans Book Club, 1964), p. 5.
3 John Sugden and Alan Tomlinson, *FIFA and the Contest for World Football: Who Rules the Peoples' Game?* (Polity Press, 1998), p. 246.

NOTES

4   The Kenya example is from Alan Tomlinson, *FIFA; The Men, the Myths and the Money* (Routledge, 2014), pp. 155–158.
5   David Goldblatt, *The Age of Football: The Global Game in the Twenty-First Century* (Macmillan, 2019), p. 82.
6   Piers Edwards and Romain Molina, 'Jailed candidate set to win Mali FA elections', *BBC*, 28 August 2023 https://www.bbc.co.uk/sport/africa/66638502, accessed 9 January 2025.
7   Saminda Kunti, 'Mali's Mamatou Touré says prison and health have forced him to quit FIFA Council', *Inside World Football*, 20 January 2025, https://www.insideworldfootball.com/2025/01/20/malis-mamatou-toure-says-prison-health-forced-quit-fifa-council/, accessed 14 July 2025.
8   Brian Oliver, 'Free-for-all and corruption in African football shames FIFA', *The Guardian*, 24 October 2010, https://www.theguardian.com/football/2010/oct/24/corruption-african-football-fifa, accessed 14 July 2025.
9   Ibid.
10 Mark Gleeson, 'Reward system', *When Saturday Comes* 452 (April 2025), p. 27.
11 Ibid.
12 Goldblatt, *The Age of Football*, p. 93.
13 Nick Ames, 'From women's team to grassroots game: Questions linger in Qatar – What is going on with the women's national team?', *The Guardian*, 30 March 2023, https://www.theguardian.com/football/2023/mar/30/from-the-womens-team-to-grassroots-football-questions-lingering-in-qatar-after-world-cup, accessed 25 July 2025.
14 Alan Tomlinson, 'Eastern promise? Football in the societies and cultures of the Middle and Far East', in Alan Tomlinson (ed), *Sport and Leisure Cultures* (University of Minnesota Press, 2005), p. 141.
15 DCMS (Department of Culture, Media and Sport), *Staging of International Sporting Events: The 2006 World Cup Campaign* (London, 8 December 2000), p. 28. Memorandum submitted by the Football Association to the House of Commons Culture, Media, and Sport Committee (document reference SF20).
16 Peter Velappan, *Asian Football in the New Millennium*, presented at media seminar held in conjunction with the 11th Asian Cup, Abu Dhabi, United Arab Emirates, 14 December 1996.
17 Peter Velappan, *Beyond Dreams: The Fascinating Story of the Blessed Life of Peter Velappan s/o Palaniappan* (Vivar Printing Sdn. Bhd., 2013), p. 191.
18 Bill Murray, 'Cultural revolution? Football in the societies of Asia and the Pacific', in Stephen Wagg (ed) *Giving the Game Away: Football, Politics and Culture on Five Continents* (Leicester University Press, 1995), pp. 138–162, at p. 138.

19 Personal interview, 29 January 2025.
20 Samindra Kunti, 'A brave new world: Saudi Arabia's takeover of world football continues apace with the upcoming FIFA World Cup', *World Soccer* (December 2023), p. 33.
21 Alan Tomlinson, 'Ego tripping', *When Saturday Comes* 450 (February 2025), pp. 30–31.
22 Chris Dalby, '18 ways in which Saudi Arabia bought the Club World Cup', *Sports and Crime Briefing*, 14 June 2025, https://www.sportsandcrime.com/p/18-ways-in-which-saudi-arabia-bought, accessed 17 June 2025.
23 Alan Tomlinson, 'No contest', *When Saturday Comes* 437 (December 2023), p. 32.

Chapter 8

1 Jill Ellis, in 'Beyond Greatness™', *inside.fifa.com*, https://inside.fifa.com/tournament-organisation/fifa-womens-world-cup-2023-tournament-recap#on-the-pitch, accessed 10 June 2025.
2 Brighton Museum & Art Gallery, *Goal Power! Women's Football 1894–2022*, exhibition 18 June–25 September 2022.
3 The Dick, Kerr Ladies story is told by Gail J. Newsham, *In a League of Their Own! The Dick, Kerr Ladies' Football Club* (Scarlet Press, 1997). Summaries and direct quotations from this revealing book are from pp. 44–50, 56, 68 and 134.
4 Personal interview (by John Sugden), 12 November 1996, Chicago, USA.
5 Jean Williams, *A Beautiful Game: International Perspectives on Women's Football* (Berg, 2007), p. 83.
6 Joseph S. Blatter, 'Editorial: The future is feminine', *FIFA News*, 6–7/95, p. 1.
7 Quoted in Marcus Christensen and Paul Kelso, 'Soccer chief's plan to boost women's game? Hotpants', *The Guardian*, 16 January 2004.
8 Grahame L. Jones. 'Blatter's comments criticized', *Los Angeles Times*, 17 January 2004.
9 Brandi Chastain, with Gloria Averbuch, *It's Not About the Bra: How to Play Hard, Play Fair, and Put the Fun Back into Competitive Sports* (HarperCollins, 2004), pp. 172–173.
10 Quoted in Jean Williams, *A Game for Rough Girls? A History of Women's Football in Britain* (Routledge, 2003), p. 116.
11 Donna de Varona, ' "M's" in football: Myths, management, marketing, media and money. A reprise', in Fan Hong and J.A. Mangan (eds) *Soccer, Women, Sexual Liberation: Kicking Off a New Era* (Frank Cass, 2004), pp. 7–13, at p. 13.
12 Ibid, p. 7.

13 Andrei S. Markovits and Steven L. Hellerman, 'Women's soccer in the United States: Yet another American "exceptionalism"', in Fan Hong and J.A. Mangan (eds) *Soccer, Women, Sexual Liberation: Kicking Off a New Era* (Frank Cass, 2004), pp. 14–29, at p. 26.
14 See FIFA's 2023 Annual Report, https://inside.fifa.com/official-documents/annual-report/2023/around-fifa/fifa-statistics, accessed 13 July 2025.
15 Brighton Museum & Art Gallery, *Goal Power!*
16 Manish Pandey and Iqra Farooq, 'Women's World Cup 2023: "Nouhaila Benzina is a role model to us"', *BBC News*, 30 July 2023, https://www.bbc.co.uk/news/newsbeat-66289236, accessed 13 June 2025.
17 Chuka Onwumechili, 'Women football players in Africa have overcome enormous barriers – new book tells the story', *The Conversation*, 4 July 2024, https://theconversation.com/women-football-players-in-africa-have-overcome-enormous-barriers-new-book-tells-the-story-231314#:~:text=In%20South%20Africa%2C%20for%20example,game%20needs%20funding%20for%20development, accessed 13 June 2025.
18 Manal Hamzeh, 'FIFA's double hijabophobia: A colonialist and Islamist alliance racializing Muslim women soccer players', *Women's Studies International Forum* 63 (2017), pp. 11–16, at p. 14.
19 CBS News, 'Iran women's soccer team thwarted by hijab ban', 7 June 2011.
20 IFAB, *The IFAB Organisation*, https://www.theifab.com/organisation/, accessed 7 July 2025.
21 Prithi Yelaja, 'Lifting of hijab ban in world soccer welcomed', *CBC News*, 6 March 2012, https://www.cbc.ca/news/world/lifting-of-hijab-ban-in-world-soccer-welcomed-1.1235718, accessed 13 June 2025.
22 Heba Kanso, 'FIFA to engage with Iran to lift ban on women in stadiums', *Iran News* (by Reuters), 9 November 2018, https://www.cbc.ca/news/world/lifting-of-hijab-ban-in-world-soccer-welcomed-1.1235718, accessed 13 June 2025.

Chapter 9

1 See Stephen Weatherill, Clarendon Law Lecture Series 2022–23 (2022), University of Oxford, https://www.law.ox.ac.uk/content/event/clarendon-law-lecture-series-2022-23, accessed 20 January 2023.
2 Professor Stephen Weatherill, Clarendon Law Lecture Series Lecture 1, presented in The Gulbenkian Lecture Theatre, Faculty of Law, University of Oxford, 14 November 2022.
3 Ken Foster, 'Developments in sporting law', in Lincoln Allison (ed) *The Changing Politics of Sport* (Manchester University Press, 1993), pp. 105–124.

4   Ibid, p. 105.
5   Ibid, p. 105.
6   Ibid, p. 122.
7   David McArdle, 'Reflections on the Harry Reynolds litigation', *Entertainment and Sports Law Journal* 2:2 (2003), pp. 90–97, at p. 95.
8   Staff and Agencies, 'FIFA unveils Coe as ethics czar', *The Guardian*, 15 September 2006.
9   Ibid.
10 David Owen, 'Exclusive: Coe replaced as head of FIFA Ethics Commission', *Inside the Games*, 17 March 2010.
11 Matt Scott, 'FIFA's new ethics code shows intention to end transparency', *ESPN*, 20 August 2018.
12 Ibid.
13 Michael Shields, 'Swiss appeals court convicts ex-FIFA official Valcke of accepting bribes', *Reuters News*, 24 June 2022.
14 These two cases were cited in E.A. Brett and Alan Tomlinson, 'Misgoverning world football: Agency and (non)accountability at FIFA', *Oxford Journal of Legal Studies* 45:1 (Spring 2025), pp. 108–137.
15 'Statement of the chairman of the FIFA Adjudicatory Chamber, Hans Joachim Eckert, on the examination of the ISL case', 29 April 2013, p. 3, https://www.sportsintegrityinitiative.com/wp-content/uploads/2015/12/islreporteckert29.04.13e.pdf, accessed 20 September 2024.
16 CNN, 'Swiss court: Former FIFA president Havelange took $1.5M in bribes', 12 July 2012, https://www.cnn.com/2012/07/11/sport/football/football-havelange-teixeira-fifa-bribes/index.html, accessed 19 September 2024.
17 These direct quotes from the Sealed Proceedings are at pp. 31, 32 and 33, see https://www.documentcloud.org/documents/2093153-blazer.html, accessed 13 March 2025.
18 Helen Jefferson Lenskyj, *Gender, Athletes' Rights, and the Court of Arbitration for Sport* (Emerald Publishing, 2018), p. 161.

Chapter 10

1   See https://inside.fifa.com/legal/integrity/news/gianni-infantino-says-fifa-and-member-associations-must-fight-match-fixing-together, accessed 7 July 2025.
2   See Annual Report 2023, https://inside.fifa.com/official-documents/annual-report/2023/financials/2023-financial-statements/notes/36-consolidated-subsidiaries, accessed 13 July 2025.

FURTHER READING

History of FIFA

Lincoln Allison and Alan Tomlinson, *Understanding International Sport Organisations: Principles, Power and Possibilities* (Routledge, 2017).

Paul Darby, *Africa, Football and FIFA: Politics, Colonialism and Resistance* (Frank Cass, 2002).

Pierre Lanfranchi, Christiane Eisenberg, Tony Mason and Alfred Wahl, *100 Years of Football: The FIFA Centennial Book* (Weidenfeld & Nicholson, 2004).

Stefan Rinke and Kay Schiller (eds), *The FIFA World Cup 1930–2010: Politics, Commerce, Spectacle and Identities* (Wallstein Verlag, 2014).

Stanley Rous, *Football Worlds: A Lifetime in Sport* (Faber & Faber, 1978).

Vyv Simson and Andrew Jennings, *The Lords of the Rings: Power, Money and Drugs in the Modern Olympics* (Simon & Schuster, 1992).

John Sugden and Alan Tomlinson, *FIFA and the Contest for World Football: Who Rules the Peoples' Game?* (Polity Press, 1998).

Alan Tomlinson, *FIFA (Fédération Internationale de Football Association): The Men, the Myths and the Money* (Routledge, 2014).

Stephen Wagg (ed), *Giving the Game Away: Football, Politics and Culture on Five Continents* (Leicester University Press, 1995).

David Yallop, *How They Stole the Game* (Poetic Publishing, 1999).

FIFA scandals

Ken Bensinger, *Red Card: FIFA and the Fall of the Most Powerful Men in Sports* (Profile Books, 2018).

Heidi Blake and Jonathan Calvert, *The Ugly Game: The Qatari Plot to Buy the World Cup* (Simon & Schuster, 2015).

E.A. Brett and Alan Tomlinson, 'Mis-governing world football: Agency and (non)accountability at FIFA', *Oxford Journal of Legal Studies* 45:1 (Spring 2025), pp. 108–137. https://doi.org/10.1093/ojls/gqae036

David Conn, *The Fall of the House of FIFA* (Yellow Jersey Press, 2017).

Andrew Jennings, *Foul! The Secret World of FIFA: Bribes, Vote Rigging and Ticket Scandals* (HarperSport, 2006).

Bonita Mersiades, *Whatever it Takes: The Inside Story of the FIFA Way* (Powderhouse Press, 2018).

Netflix, *FIFA Uncovered* (Netflix mini-series, 4 episodes, 2022).

John Sugden and Alan Tomlinson, *Football, Corruption and Lies: Revisiting 'Badfellas', the Book that FIFA Tried to Ban* (Routledge, 2017).

The women's game

Manal Hamzeh, 'FIFA's double hijabophobia: A colonialist and Islamist alliance racializing Muslim women soccer players', *Women's Studies International Forum* 63 (2017), pp. 11–16.

Fan Hong and J.A. Mangan (eds), *Soccer, Women, Sexual Liberation: Kicking Off a New Era* (HarperCollins, 2004).

Jean Williams, *A Beautiful Game: International Perspectives on Women's Football* (Berg, 2007).

Human rights and sport law

Helen Jefferson Lenskyj, *Gender, Athletes' Rights and the Court of Arbitration for Sport* (Emerald Publishing, 2018).

Dave McArdle, 'Reflections on the Harry Reynolds litigation', *Entertainment and Sports Law Journal* 2:2 (2003), pp. 90–97.

Nicholas McGeehan, Usman Jawed and Marilyn Croser, *Substitute: The Case for External Reform at FIFA* (FairSquare/fairsq.org, 2024).

INDEX

References to figures are in *italics*; references to tables and boxes are in **bold**.

1930 FIFA World Cup (Uruguay) 23, 63, **65**, 139, 140
1934 FIFA World Cup (Italy) **65**, 84, 140
1938 FIFA World Cup (France) **65**, 140, *141*
1950 FIFA World Cup (Brazil) **65**
1954 FIFA World Cup (Switzerland) **65**
1958 FIFA World Cup (Sweden) **65**
1962 FIFA World Cup (Chile) **65**
1966 FIFA World Cup (England) **65**
1970 FIFA World Cup (Mexico) **65**
1974 FIFA World Cup (West Germany) **65**
1978 FIFA World Cup (Argentina) 54, **65**, 84
1982 FIFA World Cup (Spain) **65**
1986 FIFA World Cup (Mexico) **65**, 90, 91
1990 FIFA World Cup (Italy) **65**
1991 FIFA Women's World Cup (China) 116–117
1994 FIFA World Cup (United States) 65–66, **65**, 90–95
1995 FIFA Women's World Cup (Sweden) 117–118
1998 FIFA World Cup (France) **65**, 66
1999 FIFA Women's World Cup (United States) 119–120
2002 FIFA World Cup (Japan/South Korea) **66**, 105
2006 FIFA World Cup (Germany) **66**, 106
2010 FIFA World Cup (South Africa) 30, **66**, 135
2011 FIFA Women's World Cup (Germany) 105
2014 FIFA World Cup (Brazil) *28*, *29*, **66**
2015 FIFA Women's World Cup (Canada) 105
2018 FIFA World Cup (Russia) 47, **66**, 74–75, 82–84, 130–131
2022 FIFA World Cup (Qatar) 26, **66**, 74–76, 130–131, 140–142
2023 FIFA Women's World Cup (Australia/New Zealand) 111, 122, 144
2026 FIFA World Cup (Canada/Mexico/United States) 6, 43, 61–63, **66**, 98–99, 122, 140–142

INDEX

2027 FIFA Women's World Cup (Brazil) 121, 144
2030 FIFA World Cup (Morocco/Portugal/Spain) 63, 77, 80
2031 FIFA Women's World Cup (Mexico/United States) 94, 121, 144
2034 FIFA World Cup (Saudi Arabia) 75, 77–81
2035 FIFA Women's World Cup (United Kingdom) 144–145

A

Adidas 25, 52–53, 68
Adorno, Theodor 7
African Football League 103–104, 144
Al-Hilal SFC 109
Ali bin Al Hussein, Prince of Jordan 125
Al-Khelaifi, Nasser bin Ghanim 109–110
Amnesty International 80–81
anti-racism initiatives 46, **47–48**
apartheid 24
Aramco 68
Argentina 18, 19, 61, 86, 87–88, 91
Arnold, Jon 95
Asian Cup 107
Asian Football Confederation (AFC) 38, 54, 104–107
Aston Villa FC 15
Australia 19
Austria 18

B

Barbados 29
Bardi, Giovanni de' 12
BBC World Service 102
Beckenbauer, Franz 91
Beckham, David 96
Belgium 18, 20
Benzina, Nouhaila 123–124
Blatter, Joseph Sepp 10–12, **23**, 25–31, *25*, 34, 51, 55, 58, 73, 78, 83, 92, 117–119, 129–131, 133
Blazer, Chuck 27, 133–136, *134*
Bois de Boulogne Football and Athletics Club 19
Bolivia 88
Bourdieu, Pierre 7
Bragg, Melvyn 14
Brazil 29, 61, 88, 89, 120–121
Breitenstein, Rose-Marie 40–41
bribery *see* corruption
British expats 19, 87
British Ladies' Football Club 112
Browne-Wilkinson, Sir Nicolas 128–129
Brundage, Avery 50
Buechel, Roland 145
Buenos Aires FC 19

C

calcio (Florentine ball game) 12
Canada 19, 61, 86, 95
Cañedo, Guillermo 90
Cannes Film Festival 29
Caribbean Football Union 38
Carrington, Ben 48
Cayman Islands 29
Cecil, David 50
Charles II, King of England 12
Charterhouse School 13
Chastain, Brandi 118–119
Chelsea FC 110
Chile 61, 88

165

China 10–12, 116–117
Club World Cup (CWC) 36, 89, 94, 97, 98, 104, 108–110, 122
Coca-Cola Company 53–54, 68
Coe, Sebastian 130
Colombia 61, 88, 90
commercial partnerships 49, 52–58, 67–70, 83, 143
Confederación Sudamericana de Fútbol (CONMEBOL) 33, 38, 40–41, 86, 88–89
Confédération Africaine de Football (CAF) 38, 54, 101–104
Confederation of North, Central America and Caribbean Association Football (CONCACAF) 5–6, 26–27, 29, 33, 38, 41–42, 45–46, 86–87, 89–98
continental confederations (CCs) 37–38, 40–42, 44, 48, 55, 86–87, **108**, 121, 145
corporate sponsorship 49, 52–58, 67–70, 83, 143
corruption 26–34, 56–60, 57, 72–75, 101–103, 107, 131–137, 142
Court of Arbitration for Sport 126, **127**
Credit Suisse 59–60
Cruyff, Johan 91
cuju (ancient ball game) 10–11

D

Dalby, Chris 109
Dassler, Horst 52–53, 54–56, 58–59
de Varona, Donna 119–120
Denmark 20
Depardieu, Gérard 30

Der Spiegel 30
development initiatives 42–43, 48, 120, 144
Dick, Kerr Ladies FC 113–115
Drewry, Arthur **23**

E

Eckert, Hans-Joachim 132–133, 136
Ecuador 88
Edward III, King of England 12
Edwards, Piers 102
Egypt 10, 63
England 12–18, 19, 21, 61, 106, 112–115, 138, 139, 140
equal pay 121–122
Espir, André 20
Eton College 13, 19
Eusebio 91
Everton FC 3–4

F

FairSquare 76–77, 82, 85, 143
fans 3–4, 5, 65–66, **65**, **66**, 95–96, 111, 112, 140–142
Federal Bureau of Investigation (FBI) 27, 136
Fédération Internationale de Football Association (FIFA)
   finances and budgets 10, 21, 29, 48, 56, 59–60, 66–67, 72
   formation 19–21, 139
   governance 39–40, 76–81, 77–80, 85, 142–143
   headquarters and offices 20, 21, 24, 51, **52**, 97
   internal disciplinary framework 28, 29, 129–133, 136–137
   membership 37–39

organizational
  structure 36–37
presidents 22–23, **23**
statutes 24, 39, 44, 75–76,
  145–146
transparency and
  accountability 22, 110,
  145–146
FIFA Confederations Cup 29
FIFA Congresses 23, 24, 36,
  39–40, **47**, 81, 88, 98
FIFA Ethics Committee 28, 29,
  36, 130–131
FIFA Forward 42, 43
FIFA Legal and Compliance
  Office 97
FIFA News 117
FIFA Professional Football
  Landscape 39
Fluminense FC 109
Football Association (FA) 14–15,
  19, 21, 106, 112, 114, 138–139
football supporters *see* fans
Forward Development
  Programme (Forward 3.0) 6
Foster, Ken 128, 129
France 18, 19–20, 61
Freemason's Tavern, London 14

G

Garcia, Michael 136
gay rights 76, 82, **123**
Gazprom 83
Germany 20–21, 61, 91
Gibraltar 37
Giulianotti, Richard 16
Glanville, Brian 93
Gleeson, Mark 103
globalization 60–63
Goldblatt, David 11, 61,
  83, 101
Gómez, Hector R. 88
Grafström, Mattius 77–78
grassroots football 2–3, 121
  see also development
  initiatives
Greenland 5, 45–46
The Guardian 29
Guérin, Robert 20, 21, **23**

H

Hammam, Mohamed bin 26–27
Harrow School 13, 19
Harvey, Adrian 15–16
Hassan, Asma 124
Havelange, Dr João 18, 21–22,
  23, **23**, 25–26, 25, 28, 33, 41,
  51–53, 55, 57, 59, 72–73, 90,
  91, 93, 116–117, 132–133, 136
Hayatou, Issa 101
Herren, Andreas 59–60
Hickey, Colm 15
hijabs 123–125
Hirschman, Carl 20, 21
Hoffman, Jordan 29
homophobia **123**
Honduras 29
Honeyball, Nettie 112
human rights 75–81, 82,
  107–108, 110, 136–137, 142
Human Rights Watch 107–108
Hungary 18
Hyundai/Kia 68

I

India 19
Infantino, Gianni 6, **23**,
  34–35, 42–43, 48, 61–63,
  77–80, 84, 85, 96–99,
  103–104, 108–110, 121, 125,
  131, 142, 143

Inter Miami CF 96
International Amateur Athletics Federation (IAAF) **127**, 129
International Federation of Professional Footballers (Fifpro) 144–145
International Football Association Board (IFAB) 18, 124–125
International Olympic Committee (IOC) 50, 54–55, 59, 83, **127**
International Sport and Leisure (ISL) 28, 54–59, 132–133
Iran 124–125
Irish Football Association 17, 23
Israel 44
Italy 61, 140

J

Japan 61, 63, 95, 104–105
Jennings, Andrew 27, 58–59, 73

K

Käser, Dr Helmut 72
Kaufman, Michelle 97
Kenya 101
Killeen, Al 53–54
Kunti, Samindra 107–108
Kushner, Jared 99
Kuwait 107

L

Labour Force Survey Quality Review 14
Last Week Tonight **30**
Lenovo 68
Lenskyj, Helen Jefferson 136–137
Lenz, Jürgen 58
Leoz, Nicolás 28, 132–133
Liechtenstein 58
Lipton Cup 87
Ljundqvist, Arne 129
Los Angeles Galaxy 96
Los Angeles Olympics (1984) 92
Los Angeles Times 118–119

M

Major League Soccer (MLS) 93, 95–96
Mali 102
Mamelodi Sundowns FC 103–104
Manchester City FC 109
Mangan, J.A. 15
Manning, Gustav 20
marketing rights 55–56, 57–59, 57, 67–68, 90
Markovits, Andrei 90–91
MasterCard 68–69
match-fixing 102–103, 107, 131, 142
McGeehan, Nick 76, 85
media rights 50, 52, 55–56, 57–59, 57, 67, 144
Melbourne FC 19
Mersiades, Bonita 73–74
Messi, Lionel 96
Mexico 61, 90
Miami 96–98
Montréal CF 95
Morocco 61, 80, 98, 140–142
Motsepe, Patrice 102, 103–104
Muhlinghaus, Louis 20
Munro, Bob 103
Murray, Bill 107
Muslim footballers 123–125, **123**
Mussolini, Benito 84, 140
Mutko, Vitaly 82–83

INDEX

N

Nally, Patrick 52–55
national football associations (NFAs) 14–15, 17–18, 19–21, 37, 44–45, 48, 86, 106–107
Nazer, Abdul Fatah 105–106
Nebiolo, Primo 59
Neill, Sam **30**
Netherlands 20
New York Times 98
Newsham, Gail 113
North American Soccer League (NASL) 91, 95
Northampton Town FC 15

O

The Observer 3–4, 102–103
Oceania Football Confederation 38
Oliver, Brian 102–103
Oliver, Guy 87
Oliver, John **30**
Olympic Games 23, 36, 50, 54–55, 59, 82, 83, 92, 120, 139
Oneida Football Club 19
Onwumechili, Chuka 123

P

Paraguay 61, 88
Paris Olympics (2024) 120
Paris Saint-Germain FC 109–110
Pelé 91
Peru 88
Platini, Michel 34
political neutrality 44, 83
Portugal 61, 80
Premier League 95–96
Preska, Judge Loretta 68–69
public protests 28–29, *28*, 83
public school influence 13–16
Putin, Vladimir 82

Q

Qatar 61, 75, 76, 84, 95, 105, 106, 107
Qatar Airways 68
Queen's Park FC 17–18

R

racism 46, **47–48**, **123**
Racketeer Influenced and Corrupt Organizations Act (US) 32
Radnege, Keir 37
Rapinoe, Megan 121–122
Real Madrid CF 10, 20, 109
Reynolds, Butch 129
Rimet, Jules 21, **23**, 24, 60
Roth, Tim **30**
Rothenberg, Alan 92–93, *94*, 120
Rouhani, Hassan 125
Rous, Sir Stanley 12, 21, **23**, 24, 38, 40–41, 50–51, 72, 89–90, 100
Rugby Football Union 13
Rugby School 13–14, 19
Ruggie, John 71
Russia 44, 61, 82–84

S

Saltley Stallions FC 124
Samaranch, Juan Antonio 55
Samoura, Fatma **47**, 125
San Diego FC 96
Saraswathi, Vani 84
Saudi Arabia 61, 63, 75, 77–81, 99, 104–106, 107–110

Schneider, Viktor 20
Scotland 17–18, 23
Seeldrayers, Rodolphe William 23
Shakespeare, William 12
Sheffield Wednesday FC 15
Simelane, Eudy **123**
Soccer United Marketing 96
Sochi Winter Olympics (2014) 82, 83
Sonntagsblick 118
Soumara, Fatma 102
South Africa 21, 24, 61, 95, **123**, 135
South Korea 61, 95, 104–105, 140–142
Spain 20, 29, 61, 80, 140
spectators 3–4, 5, 65–66, **65**, **66**, 95–96, 111, 112, 125, 140–142
sports law 126–137, **127**
sports marketing bribery schemes *see* corruption
Sports Rights Alliance 81
Steinbrecher, Hank 116, **117**
Stockholm Olympics (1912) 23
Stoke City FC 15
Strange, Susan 48–49
Sulser, Claudio 130
Sweden 20, 61
Switzerland 20, 61
Sylow, Ludwig 20

T

Talbot, Margaret 119
Talent Development Scheme 43
television rights 50, 52, 55–56, 57–59, **57**, 67, 144
Texeira, Ricardo 132–133
Thailand 63
Title IX legislation (US) 116

Tom Brown's Schooldays (Hughes) 19
Topping, Alexandra 3–4
Toronto FC 95
Touré, Mammoth 102
Trinidad and Tobago 29
Trump, Donald 43, 98–99, 110

U

Ukraine 44, 82
Unión Centroamericana de Fútbol 38
Union des sociétés françaises de sports athlétiques (USFSA) 20
Union of European Football Associations (UEFA) 38, 43–44, 45, 58, 89
United Arab Emirates 105, 107
United Passions: The True Story of the World Cup 30
United Soccer League 96
United States 5–6, 19, 61, 65–66, 86, 90–98, 115–116, 120
United States Soccer Federation (USSF) 92, 93, 96, 116, **117**, 122
University of Cambridge 13–14
University of Oxford 13
Uruguay 18, 61, 63, 86, 87–88
US Department of Justice (DoJ) 27–28, 32, *33*, 56

V

Valcke, Jérôme 69, 131–132
Vancouver FC 95
Vanuatu 42–43
Velappan, Peter 106–107
Venezuela 88
Visa 68, 69

W

Wales 17, 23
Walsall FC 15
Warner, Jack 26–27
Watson Hutton, Alexander 87
Weatherill, Stephen 126–128
Weber, Jean-Marie 56–57, 73
Wenger, Arsène 43
Westminster School 13
Whitehead, Edwin 114–115
Wilson, Jonathan 79
Winterbottom, Walter 100
Wolverhampton Wanderers FC 15
Women's Football Association 115
women's game 36, 105, 111–125, **117**, **123**, 144–145
women's rights 112–115, 122–125, **123**, 142
Woolfall, Daniel Burley 21, **23**, 88, 139
worker exploitation 76, 80–81, 142
World Athletics Championships 59
World Athletics (formerly IAAF) **127**, 129
World Cup bidding processes 26, 48, 74–75, 77–81, 84–85, 90, 98–99, 106, 130–131
World Cup venues 61–63, 62, 81–82
World Cup winners 64
world ranking system 42, 88–89
World Soccer 92
Wydad AC 103–104

Z

Zenit St Petersburg FC 83